Praise for *Born To Succeed*

'Clear and concise, well-structured and learned.'
Sunday Independent

'Compulsory reading for anyone who aims to succeed.'
Dr Marilyn Orcharton, Founder, Denplan.

'The best book on personal effectiveness I have ever read.'
Les O'Reilly, Chairman, The Database Group

'Creates positive results for personal and business success.'
Evening Standard

'This book is a must for deciding what you want and how to achieve it.'
Vera Peiffer, bestselling author of *Positive Thinking*

'Success in business is about releasing our potential. This is the definitive guide to doing just that.'
Ken Moran, Chairman, Pfizer UK

COLIN TURNER

THE
EUREKA
PRINCIPLE

Alternative Thinking
for
Personal and Business Success

ELEMENT
Shaftesbury, Dorset • Rockport, Massachusetts
Melbourne, Victoria

© Element Books Limited 1995
Text © Colin Turner 1995

First published in Great Britain in 1995 by
Element Books Limited

This edition
published in Great Britain in 1997 by
Element Books Limited
Shaftesbury, Dorset SP7 8BP

Published in the USA in 1997 by
Element Books, Inc.
PO Box 830, Rockport, MA 01966

Published in Australia in 1997 by
Element Books
and distributed by Penguin Books Australia Limited
487 Maroondah Highway, Ringwood,
Victoria 3134

Cover design by Dick Evry, Create
Text design by Roger Lightfoot
Text illustrations by Richard Pearce
Typeset by WestKey Limited, Falmouth, Cornwall
Printed and bound in Great Britain by
Redwood Books Ltd, Trowbridge, Wiltshire

British Library Cataloguing in Publication
data available

Library of Congress Cataloging in Publication
data available

Library of Congress Cataloguing in Publication Data
Turner, Colin
The Eureka principle: alternative thinking for
personal and business success/Colin Turner.
Includes index
1. Success in business. 2. Success.
I. Title
HF5386. T853 1995
650.1–dc20 95–9553

ISBN 1–86204–101–6

To the *True* You

CONTENTS

SPECIAL THANKS

To my wife Sharon who has lived with every line of this book, on the page and in our life together; thanks for your tolerance and perceptive wisdom. To the immensely talented Richard Pearce for illustrating my ideas in cartoon form so effectively; thanks for keeping to the deadlines. Thanks to everyone at Element and in particular Julia McCutchen for keeping me to deadlines. Thanks to all the salespeople at Penguin, without whom this philosophy would remain silent. Thanks to all those organizations who have embraced the ideas of the Eureka Principle so enthusiastically. And to my children: Jason, Dylan, Caleb and Shamira; thanks for your love, for being your own people and being my best friends.

PREFACE: A Sense of ...

This book is guaranteed to be thought-provoking. It has not been written to persuade or cajole you with a host of examples or reasoning. Any change of thinking must come from within you in order to be effective.

Take time to think about all the ideas and principles. If you disagree with a point just ignore it. Use what you do agree with to stimulate you to become your own catalyst to improve the quality of your life.

The underlying philosophy is simple: be yourself. To the degree that you are and that you align yourself to natural principles, you become increasingly receptive to the constant flow of insight that is available to all of us.

The flashes of inspiration that guide you are no longer rare when you are in tune with yourself and Universal laws. Realizing that the security and strength we seek outside of us is available internally is the essence of the Eureka Principle.

With increased understanding and awareness we can address the very source of why we think and act the way we do. This is important as what is common practice is not always common sense, but we continue to do something until we are aware of that 'sense' ourselves.

When we sense something deeper we start the process that culminates in a 'Eureka!' This is the type of insight we experience when we finally see something we thought was not there.

It's the feeling of 'Wow, that's it, I've got it!' And the stronger our beliefs are bound, the stronger the 'Eureka' feeling we experience.

The seven chapters that follow will all provide a 'sense' of something, depending upon what is currently important in your life. It may be a sense of belonging, a sense of purpose, or a sense of who you really are. Whatever it is, you will receive your own enlightenment and this will make it lasting.

FIRST: A Sense of …

PERCEPTION

There are Universal Principles which are as essential to Life's fulfilment as the gravity principle is to its survival. You do not control your life, principles do, and the degree to which you align yourself to these fundamental Laws is in direct proportion to the quality of life you receive. By establishing values which are aligned to solid principles and by crystallizing them into a personal mission you will have a sense of belonging and purpose. You will enjoy stability and growth in all your relationships with others. You will no longer have a sense of emptiness when your goals are achieved. The creativity and innovative ideas that bring positive rewards will come to you with increased regularity. There will be a sense of meaning and you will enjoy greater fulfilment in both your personal and business relationships as the same principles apply to all spheres of your life.

The way we perceive the world governs our expectations. It creates prejudices. It can distort our beliefs and make us see things that simply are not there. It makes us cynical, sceptical. But what if our fundamental perceptions are wrong and we are not prepared to test them because we have always done something in a certain manner? Much of our heritage has conditioned us to respond in a historical rather than a functional manner. When asked why we have done something in a certain way, we tend to reply 'because of this' or 'because of that' rather than 'in order to achieve this or that'. The consequence of this way of thinking is that, at detriment to ourselves, we tend to view the future merely as an extension to the past. Anything that does not fit in with our preconditioned way of thinking is rejected.

Everything in the universe is in a continuous state of evolution and is therefore in an atmosphere of change. The world is continuously changing and the way that we see the world, not in the visual but in the perceptive sense, is the way it is. In order to change our world we have to change the way we perceive it. The only constants are the Universal Laws and Principles which provide stability within growth and change. It follows that by understanding how these laws control us, and applying them for ourselves, we can learn how to move on to greater things – success, achievement, growth and balance, all the things we want out of life.

Frames of Reference

The understanding and alignment of principles is crucial to personal and business growth. First it is important to address the way we each perceive our world. We all have a frame of reference through which we interpret what we experience. The perceptive 'filter' through which all incoming information passes has been shaped by our conditioning, to the point that we only see what we expect to see. The process of perceiving involves matching 'external' jigsaw pieces with an internal picture, model or frame of reference which has been created from previous memories, experiences and conditioning. We don't passively see the world, we actively construe it. We react to situations with our own 'rules', which are often prejudiced but in accordance with our expectations.

To illustrate this point, picture the 'male chauvinist pig' driving his open-top sports car. On a bend in the road he meets an oncoming 'woman driver' swerving all over the road. They are about to collide when his quick-thinking evasive action avoids an accident. She swerves too and as she passes him she shouts out through her open window 'Pig!'. He is furious and quickly reacts with 'Cow!' and is delighted to have delivered this retort before she is out of earshot. Pleased with himself he flies round the bend and crashes into a live pig in the middle of the road.

He reacted with his own rules. He did not bother to question their accuracy as he was unaware of them. We are too. His beliefs had formed the rules that were instrumental in determining how he saw the world. If our frame of reference is inaccurate, we will continue to have strong reactions to change in our lives,

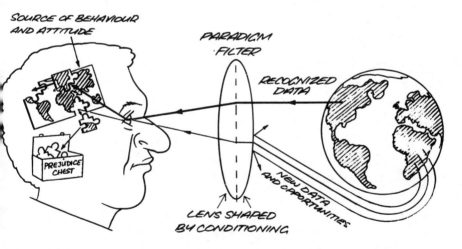

SOURCE OF BEHAVIOUR AND ATTITUDE

PARADIGM FILTER

RECOGNIZED DATA

PREJUDICE CHEST

NEW DATA AND OPPORTUNITIES

LENS SHAPED BY CONDITIONING

DATA WHICH DOES NOT 'FIT' WITH OUR PRECONDITIONED IDEAS IS FILTERED OR 'REJECTED WITH PREJUDICE' and any new incoming ideas will only end up in our 'prejudice chest'. Our 'filters' dramatically affect our thinking and judgement by influencing our perceptions. They are 'paradigms', to use the more scientific term, that form the very source of our attitudes and behaviours. The scientist Thomas Kuhn started to use the terms 'paradigm' and 'paradigm shift' in his seminal work on deep mindsets in science, *The Structure of Scientific Revolutions*. Paradigms are important because they create the lens through which we view the world, and the power in a paradigm shift is the crucial element for major change conducive to growth. Effectively, our paradigms are the models, or frames of reference or 'maps', that we use for guidance.

Stephen Covey, in his book *The Seven Habits of Highly Effective People*, underlines their importance by using the example of a misleading street map. If I sent you to Chicago with a street map of Detroit, inadvertently marked Chicago, you would be lost. If you had attended behavioural training courses then you would simply get lost quicker because of your diligent behaviour. And if you had attended positive thinking training courses, although lost you simply would not feel bad about it. But the fact is, you would still be lost. Imagine the enormous improvements you could make in your effectiveness by addressing your paradigms, the actual source of your behaviours and attitudes.

By working solely on your attitudes and behaviours you will achieve only minor advances in growth. And these are not sufficient on their own.

**To be a leader in your particular field
you have to be able to perceive
what is going to happen before it does.**

This will enable you to respond proactively and not reactively to change, which will now be accepted as a necessary prerequisite for growth. New ideas invariably cause change, inevitably cause uncertainty, and often involve more work. But the mindset that regards the future as merely an extension to the past must be reset. A mindset simply means a fixed and predominant way of thinking and seeing, and it continuously strengthens itself as we make sense of our world in ways that support those assumptions or beliefs. Our attitudes and behaviours are the outgrowth of those assumptions to the point that we think the way we see the situation '*is*' the situation. Each of us *assumes* that the way we see things is the way they are. How appropriate that this word breaks down into *ass, u* and *me* .

By actually studying the 'paradigm filters' through which we see our world, we will be able to start seeing those ideas and opportunities that we overlooked before. Where there are paradigms or models of reference, be they correct or incorrect, they will form the foundations on which we base our beliefs. Consequently, whenever others disagree with us, we immediately assume that something is wrong with them. I am sure we can all remember times when we felt that someone who did not agree with our ideas or beliefs was, well, wrong.

The Paradigm Shift

We can use the phrase 'paradigm shift' to describe situations where previous ways of seeing, thinking and behaving are no longer deemed appropriate. Some paradigm shifts are instantaneous, as in the example of the man crashing into the pig, while others can be slow and deliberate.

A change in our ideas is usually brought about not solely by 'will' but by other ideas, different levels of thinking. A 'Eureka' experience occurs when new light is suddenly shed on something familiar. New ideas take time to seep into our understanding before we can fully perceive them as our own. Often when we first hear of something new we retort 'I cannot accept that as it conflicts with my preconceived ideas.' The second time we hear it we say 'I can see what they mean, but I just can't accept it.' The third exposure may elicit 'You know, I agree with that way of thinking, although I have some reservations as to its use.' Eventually it clicks into place and we exclaim: 'That is exactly how I feel about the subject.' The more firmly fixed our beliefs, perceptions and values, the stronger the feeling we experience when a different picture is pointed out to us.

Our internal maps are drawn from information that we have previously received and from our experience and conditioning. They thus provide us with various mindsets or paradigms for all our interpretations throughout life. These models, or patterns of thinking, have their own set of rules which establish

boundaries for us and how we can be successful within those boundaries. As these paradigms act as filters which screen all information coming into our mind, new data that does not compare with our expectations is ignored.

We can literally become incapable of perceiving new data. Until we experience a change in our mindset, or a paradigm shift, our existing boundaries prevent us seeing new markets, strategies and ideas. Throughout history it has been proved that any courageous breakthrough has been a break with tradition-ally accepted thought. At these times the 'rules' are broken at the edges of accepted ways of doing things, usually by outsiders who have nothing to lose and can see things with new eyes and expectations.

A paradigm shift is experienced in the same way that in physics a body will maintain a certain direction until another body causes it to change direction. As soon as this happens, new boundaries and new horizons can be viewed, because when the rules change everyone goes back to the same point. The past guarantees nothing if the rules change.

For centuries the set boundaries of the world provided a map which perceived it to be flat. When the paradigm was shifted to accepting that the world was round – by breaking with tradition and sailing west instead of east – an enormous breakthrough in thinking was made. When Copernicus shifted the paradigm from Ptolemy's theory (that the earth was the centre of the universe and did not move) to his own (that the sun was at the centre with the earth in motion) his views were considered heresy. His conclusions were mostly hidden under Vatican lock and key for centuries as they shook the existing perceived map of heaven and earth.

When Galileo confirmed the theory, and indeed shifted the paradigm further to embrace the idea that the sun was not the centre but only a part of an infinite universe, he was threatened with imprisonment and death. Those that break with tradition start the revolutions that bring about new thinking and new boundaries necessary for growth. But, as with all revolutions, they are strongly resisted in order to maintain the status quo.

Newtonian physics shifted the boundaries yet again, so did Einstein. Both accepted that you cannot embrace a new paradigm until you let go of the old one, and that you will not see new ways while utilizing old rules and traditional formulas. The longer an accepted paradigm has been in existence, the more difficulty or crisis is felt on breaking with it. Many centuries of thinking confronted Copernicus and the revolution he was proposing. The cry went up: 'If that is the case why hasn't someone thought of it before?' The strength of a theory increases with time – and the longer the time, the less likely it is to be questioned. This often-used basis for non-acceptance of a new way of thinking has its foundations in the length of time an old thought has had to become traditional. Once this does happen, the idea rests comfortably on the individual who then feels resistance to change.

Fixed paradigms or mindsets can equip us very badly to deal with change. In the same way that armies are trained to fight the last and not the next war, many individuals and companies become fixed in yesterday's pattern of thought. In 1916 alcohol licensing laws were introduced for the sole purpose of ensuring that ammunition workers could keep to their strict work schedules and duties. After the war the paradigm stuck, and for 70 years dictated the social drinking habits of a whole nation. Some establishments still rigidly stick to the status quo, not necessarily for commercial reasons but for 'traditional' reasons. New laws allowing children to sit in public bars – about to be implemented in the UK at the time of writing – will make many feel most uncomfortable. The current mindset of splitting families up or allocating them to remote inhospitable rooms is hardly conducive to combining family and social values.

The layout of keys on a typewriter in the 'Qwerty' fashion was purposefully done over a hundred years ago in order to slow down a typist and prevent the keys jamming. However, throughout the development of electric and electronic typewriters and state-of-the-art computers, the same layout has prevailed. Despite test results which show that alternative layouts are easier to learn, create less operator fatigue and, of course, permit faster typing, the traditional layout persists. Inertia and resistance to change have been formidable obstacles in this instance.

Next time you hear yourself saying something in a traditional vein, whether it be 'that's the way it is around here' or 'just get on with it', ask yourself if you are inadvertently providing a barrier to a new individual's opportunity to improve something. If on the other hand you hear yourself say 'Things aren't what they used to be', ask yourself if you are suffering from a stuck paradigm. The 'good old days' or 'a better future' is not where your life is at. It is here, right now in the present moment. You must become aware of how your paradigms dramatically affect your actions. New thinking means seeking new ground, not breaking more old ground.

Most new ideas have been started by a solitary shout, hardly heard above the noise of ridicule and laughter, which finally becomes a crescendo due to the increasing amount of people who eventually see what the lone individual is advocating.

Einstein wrote of his 'new paradigm': 'It was as if the ground had been pulled out from under one, with no firm foundation to be seen anywhere upon which one could have built.' A perceptive historian, Hanson, described it as 'picking up the other end of the stick', the process that involves 'handling the same bundle of data as before, but placing them in a new system of relations with one another by giving them a different framework'. This can be likened to visual gestalt when two individuals see different pictures while viewing the same image. Each one is considered by the other to be wrong or, in the case of understanding something, to have the 'wrong end of the stick'.

There are 5 billion people on this planet, all perceiving things through their own unique interpretations. This implies that there are 5 billion ways of looking at things. If one group sees something and another group sees something different, does this make one of the groups wrong? And if so which group?

Look at the following caricature of a young person's profile. How old is he? What else can you say about him?

Now what if someone were to say to you that it was not a picture of a young boy at all but in fact they saw an old woman? If you were unable to see a different picture you would start to create certain opinions about the other person's way of viewing things, particularly if he or she could not see what you were seeing. The young boy's cheek and jaw are the old woman's nose and his ear is her eye. Now you can see both images, but every time you look at it in the future the image you will see first will be the young boy. Why? Because the young boy's image met with what you expected to see from the instruction you were given prior to first seeing it. (The drawing is derived from the famous 'ambiguous lady', used in psychology and gestalt principles and originally drawn by W T Hill in 1914.)

Until we are able to drop unwarranted assumptions about others and prejudices on new ideas, we cannot expect to bring about lasting improvements in our interpersonal relationships or organizations. We actively construe our world by utilizing past experience and data that are instrumental in our thinking process. In fact often the price we pay for experience is the development of a fixed way of thinking about and viewing the world.

The magic eye craze, which has so taken the nation by storm, provides an example of how we can use our visual sense in a totally different way. Yet if we were not given any indication of what could be seen we would never think to look beyond what is seemingly a colourful and uniform picture. To discover that 'hidden' picture without any frame of reference would be meaningless unless our paradigm was one of investigation and desire to seek something different. Our thinking can come completely unstuck unless we have a frame of reference or map in our experience to utilize. Look at the following picture. Can you make head or tail of it?

When you have no pattern of experience or memories to help you construe a picture you remain in an 'unstuck' state. As soon as a picture is pointed out to you, you lose that unstuckness and become fixed in what you see and in your way of thinking and how you construe a picture. If I give you a frame of reference, in this case a cow's face looking at you, after a while you will start to assimilate the information into what you expect to see. Do you see how quickly we create a mindset of seeing things and other people? New ideas are missed as we almost actively, although subconsciously, become non-receptive to that which does not comply with our own rules, boundaries or grids of reference. Do you also see the other cow in the distance? Or perhaps you saw that first.

We behave according to what we each bring to a situation and we adjust the world to suit our attitudes. As you read the following statement count the number of letter 'f's.

Fred Flintstone's popularity is a result
of years of frolicking humour and continues
to provide pleasure to people of all ages.

How many did you count? Replies usually range between one and five, with three being the most common. But there are actually six. Well done if you spotted them all the first time! But the reason why many don't see six is because their grid of reference screens out the ones in the word 'of'. We all suffer from scotomata or blind spots and in this instance we tend to read phonetically, scanning for sound. Thus we miss three 'f's by seeing 'ov' in place of 'of'.

There is no trick involved here. We all know that we agree with ourselves when so often others disagree. Yet the picture is the same for everyone. It is only our reference grid that interprets it differently. We notice what supports our expectations and ignore the rest. If, for example, someone comes up with a great idea, let's call it a 'six-f programme', but when it is shown to you all you can see is a three-f programme, what is going to be your opinion of them? Which prejudice chest will you put them in? Are they rocking the boat? Are they wrong or just being stupid?

The important point to understand is that the world does not change after a paradigm shift or a 'Eureka!' experience, but you operate in a different world afterwards. When Aristotle and Galileo looked at swinging stones, the first saw constrained fall, the second a pendulum. The principles involved in the creation of a process exist regardless of their interpretation. The 'f's are written regardless of whether you see them or not. New opportunities and ideas are accepted regardless of your understanding and perception of them.

As the set paradigms you hold are the actual source of all your behaviours and attitudes, then the leap in your effectiveness led by a new paradigm will be enormous. Your existing attitudes and behaviour skills will automatically improve as their very source, the new paradigm, causes them to adopt new rules and methods and to look at fresh opportunities. Consequently, in the fast-changing global marketplace, new entrepreneurial companies who are not constrained by the rules spawned by traditional paradigms or mindsets will shake the very foundations of those who are constrained and who will inevitably have to follow the new rules.

We know from experience that we are highly selective of evidence that supports our sense of view and blinds us to contradictory evidence. We buy a new car and immediately notice the same make and style everywhere, whereas we had previously thought it was unusual. The fact is that once our mind is set we are very quick to notice all supporting evidence.

Recognizing a Paradigm

If, as I say, we are unaware of our particular mindsets, how do we change them? In order to change them we must first recognize that we have them. Only through this awareness can we address them and, if necessary or required, cause a change or shift in them. One of the aims of this book is to stimulate your thinking in order to make you more receptive, in itself a key to changing mindsets.

First it is important to accept that your mindsets do affect you, that you can suffer as well as grow with them, and that they can be an impediment to development and achievement. Next you have to look into areas of your life where you experience a discomfort. Wherever there is a discomfort in either your personal or business life, you are suffering from a fixed paradigm, and unless you address the mindset that formalizes the process you will continue to have a recurrence of that discomfort. Blaming a system is the paradigm of 'the workman blaming his tools'. Addressing the process or system is not sufficient for improvement, it is only providing a bandage and not setting the bone. For systems and processes to improve, the thinking that formalized them must be improved.

If you are rushing between home and business, keeping all

the plates spinning and generally feeling exhausted, the discomfort will not be eased by changing your schedule. Its focus will merely shift to a feeling of guilt about not doing what you think you should be doing. Only by addressing your current paradigm in this area will a solution be forthcoming. Trying to keep everyone happy, sticking to your responsibilities and generally doing what is expected of you can often result in discomfort – you are thoroughly unhappy, everyone else is dissatisfied, and you are still wondering what it is all about. You can organize yourself until you are blue in the face but if the process you use is not in harmony with the process of Universal Laws, the exercise is short lived.

Often a crisis starts with disillusionment, a sign that a paradigm is becoming blurred and a new one forming. It is not until we question our faith, for example, that we can enjoy a greater spiritual understanding and increase our awareness in this area. To doubt something is to question it, and when we question something this helps us to crystallize our thinking on a particular subject. New horizons and boundaries assist us in developing a deeper perspective about ourselves in relation to the rest of the universe and its laws. Generally, a crisis can help you to adopt a different way of thinking or viewpoint, and from this stance you can develop newer and more appropriate rules. It's not so much that your current rules for doing things are obsolete, but more a case that they may no longer be sufficient.

Many current systems formed by an existing paradigm cause imbalance, and subsequently discomfort, in our personal and business life. All of us suffer from an expediency factor. We want things that are immediate. When we decide that we want a particular skill, relationship or possession, we want it now. We don't want to wait. Consequently we are attracted to 'quick fix' approaches that promise an immediate result. We learn how to make the right impressions, how to manipulate, how to create the desired reaction, how to put on the charm – all personality improvement techniques designed to manipulate, to get what we want, to win, to feel good about ourselves. But do we in the long term? All may be successful in the short term, but is it sustainable? Can we be efficient in building a long-term relationship or in developing our character?

Problems in our life come when we are sowing one thing and expecting to reap something entirely different. Many of our fundamental paradigms and the processes and habits that grow out of them will never produce the results we have been led to expect. These paradigms, created by people looking for a short cut, are based on a demand for a quick fix success through a good personality and are fundamentally flawed. This in turn affects not only our awareness of our fundamental needs but also the way in which we attempt to meet them.

Our lives are controlled by fundamental principles. The law of nature operates on a system based on principles, whereas the law of society is a system based on values which are often not aligned to principles. What about a paradigm from your own experience? Did you ever leave all your school revision until the last minute? Did you ever work out the system, decide what questions would come up? Did you then study like crazy to get the pass you needed? Maybe you got the qualifications but did you get the education? Was the year's work that you completed in two weeks retained with a deep understanding? Did it provide you with the ability to think creatively? Did it give you the ability to communicate effectively in writing and speech and to solve problems in improved ways?

What about your physical health? Can you overcome years of relaxed comfortable living by working out furiously two days before an event? Can you suddenly do 30 press-ups for a bet when asked to? What about your marriage or your children? Can you solve all interpersonal dilemmas by being efficient with your loved ones? What about character? Can you become a person of integrity, courage and compassion overnight?

In the short term we may be able to enjoy apparent success by going for the quick fix, but in the long term the law of nature governs all areas of our life.

We live in a modern society which leans towards short-cut techniques. The quality of life, however, cannot be achieved by taking the right short cut.

While we do have the power to choose our actions, we do not have power over the consequences of our choices. Universal Laws and Principles do. Much frustration in life would diminish if we understood that we are not in control of our lives, principles are. This paradigm shift in thinking would resolve most personal and interpersonal dilemmas within weeks. The desired outcomes would take as long as was necessary, depending on what was required, and could be months, years or even decades. An increased feeling of balance through awareness and conscience would displace the feeling of frustration felt in the past.

Is Efficient Sufficient?

Aligning your thinking to principles means focusing on doing the right things and not just doing things right. It means focusing on what is important in your life as opposed to attending to what is urgent. It means being effective as opposed to being efficient. The efficiency paradigm of getting more done in less time – increased productivity and less waste – seems to make good sense. But productivity is meaningless without goals. If you are going in one direction, no matter how efficiently, you are not being effective if it is the wrong direction. When children, spouses or colleagues open up to share something which is troubling them, what do you do if you have an urgent call to make or go to in ten minutes? As your mind cannot be fully on what they are saying, do you utilize the listening skills that you have learned in your personality training? Do you quickly suggest something from your experience to solve their upset? This may be efficient but does it create a bond? On your deathbed will you wish you had spent more time at the office? Can you believe that you will find the power to create a better quality of life in your daily planner?

You cannot separate what you do from what you are. Personal and family values are a microcosm of organizational values. You cannot effectively create a better quality of life in one area while merely being efficient in another. The same principles apply to developing character as to developing professional competence. We cannot be a law unto ourselves. The values that drive our choices, whether security, status, money, recognition or love, do not necessarily create quality results, particularly when they are in opposition to the natural laws that govern peace of mind and quality of life.

While you can be efficient with things you cannot be efficient, effectively, with people. Our paradigms lead us to what we do with our attitudes and behaviours. And what we do leads to the results we get in our lives. So if we want to create significant changes in the results we are currently getting, we cannot simply change the methods or techniques we are using as the paradigm will simply overpower and overrule the changes.

Businesses which hope to instil a culture of empowerment are unsuccessful. You cannot instil or change a culture with a quick fix, it has to be grown. Business and family cultures are manifestations of the way people think and feel. If people think one thing and do another, then their culture will quite simply be duplicitous. If there is one set of rules for 'us' and another for 'them', an atmosphere of trust will not prevail. Empowerment will never work without trust, and if trust is not developed, which can only be done through unifying principles, then the old paradigm of control overcomes the empowered behaviours and attitude-instilled methods.

Trust forms the foundation of all lasting relationships. Trust itself is an outgrowth of an individual's trustworthiness. The two key ingredients of trustworthiness are integrity and competence. For instance, if you went to someone for advice – it may be a doctor, lawyer, colleague, family member or friend – and the person was very honest but not exactly competent, then you would not entirely trust him or her to perform your request. If on the other hand this person was very competent but lacked integrity, similarly you would not be fully confident. Integrity itself is an outgrowth of character development – you cannot pretend to be honest. The long term will find you out. Competency is an outgrowth of professional development – you cannot pretend, as again the long term will find you out.

Life Is Not Divisible

What is true of character is also true of competence. To separate them is to create an illusion and to live within that illusion is incredibly strenuous. Life is one indivisible whole. You cannot put on personality clothes to role play in one area of your life and then present a different facade for another area. Wearing a work hat, a social hat and a home hat creates imbalance. Doing this is like that last-minute revision – you get by but don't develop. As the same principles apply in all areas of life, a more holistic paradigm is required if we are to obtain the balance which in itself makes such an enormous difference in our lives.

Balance is not achieved by jumping between compartments. It is living your life as one whole interrelated compartment. When you focus on principles, different hats, roles and compartments are no longer segmented. The internal synergy created from interrelated compartments provides increased energy and well-being. You literally are empowering yourself first.

Empowerment must be developed from the inside out. Only by developing yourself in this way can you build up a solid substance of character, rich in integrity and maturity. This deep, non-superficial kind of character is essential to provide lasting solutions to life's problems. A cosmetic personality providing quick fix solutions cannot solve the deep fundamental problems we face, even though they were created on a superficial level. This latter, more dominant, social paradigm is rooted in the 'outside-in' approach, when people blame their situations on external circumstances and conditions. It is a mindset fixed to see everything in scarcity as opposed to abundance.

On a personal level, if we have this fixed paradigm we can work on our behaviour or attitude but we will only see a certain amount of time for each of the 'hats' that we have to wear or the roles we play. If one area wins then another must lose. With this thinking we compete with ourselves. When what we think becomes a self-fulfilling prophecy we rationalize the evidence to justify the position we find ourselves in. On an interpersonal level, we see ourselves competing with others. If someone has more of something, then we must have less. When a competitor enjoys success we feel cheated or that we have lost an opportunity – and certainly that there is now less. When an associate, friend, or even family member does well and receives an accolade, we may be delighted on the outside but secretly we are wishing it could have been us. This social paradigm causes us to see situations in win or lose or, at best, compromise terms. Our thinking is scripted into 'either/or', never 'and' or, put simply, 'win/win'. We think this is too unrealistic to even be considered.

Transcending Existing Thinking

We need a new level of thinking, a character-based approach that is drawn from Universal Principles. It is self-defeating to continue in a practice simply because you have always done so, if the practice has not grown out of fundamental principles.

If you carry on doing what you have always done, you will carry on getting what you have always got.

Building character strength is like building physical strength. When the test comes, if you don't have it, no cosmetics can disguise the fact that it just isn't there. You can't fake it. You carry on reaping what you have sown no matter how many quick fixes you attempt.

Principles are immovable. They don't break, but you can break against them. Principles of character develop responsible, competent and trustworthy individuals: individuals who are proactive not reactive and internally driven by their various interrelated roles, values and missions; individuals who refuse to be externally influenced and controlled by social practices; individuals who enjoy an abundance mentality, a mentality that sees more of everything and enjoys boundless opportunity; individuals who see win/win situations as the norm, where the success and growth of one person is not interpreted as a corresponding failure or loss for another; individuals who do not feel that their own success is precluded when they hear of another's.

An abundance mentality springs from an internal security, not from possessions, associations, opinions or comparisons. Those who derive their security from external sources become dependent on them, and as scarcity thinkers believe that resources are diminished when another gets or receives something they want, their security is threatened. The only security comes from the soul of the individual, from an understanding, thinking and acceptance of personal responsibility. The continuing process of character development through self-awareness, evaluation, and conscience creates an upwardly spiralling growth of learning and expansion, which leads to progressively higher levels of effectiveness and achievement.

By transcending your existing paradigms with an alternative more holistic paradigm, the improvements in both your effectiveness and productivity will be enormous. By having the appropriate map, template, or fundamental framework for thinking, you will find that the attitudes and behaviours affecting your actions will automatically improve. As your paradigms dramatically influence your perceptions, by addressing them you will dramatically improve your effectiveness in your communications with others.

Further, by establishing a paradigm based on principles you will be able to align your own beliefs, values and mission with those of your business, thereby creating a greater spirit of harmony. In this atmosphere your intuitive ideas will increase in their regularity and your creativity will flow faster. Once an atmosphere of tension spawned from hidden agendas, back-biting and in-house politics is replaced with an atmosphere of trust and synergy, the innovation required for continuous growth is increased.

With new boundaries more effective ways of evaluating ourselves and others can be developed. Better methods of communication can be worked out and effective ways of improving our strengths and those of others can be achieved. Upon this framework a personal mission providing a sense of belonging can be established. Horizons can be constantly stretched providing a greater challenge for yet further development. The heights you can grow to are infinite when you have a solid foundation – a recognized principle that is not always followed. Life is a process and as processes flow from principles it is now important to establish exactly what principles are.

SECOND: A Sense of ...

PRINCIPLE

In its Latin derivation and its Greek root equivalent, principle means the 'beginning' or 'foundation'. In general any principle that we appeal to in resolving a problem, or in deciding our actions, can be applied again and again in other circumstances. In addition to this general characteristic, principles also have the quality of being the underlying origin or source from which a set of consequences follow. Principles and causes are the same. The word principle merely signifies that from which something proceeds.

Principle and Process

The particular state of someone's character, be it deep or shallow, strong or weak, is the consequence of a foundational cause. The how and what are the principle and process, and are inseparable. Whatever you create in your life is a process, and its harmony or turbulence will be according to how strictly the underlying principle is adhered to. The whole of creation is a process and the same principles apply in society as they do in nature. Natural laws and rules are an outgrowth of principles. But whereas natural laws are uniform, man-made conventions and laws are variable, because of our power of choice, and are not always an outgrowth of principles. More often they are simply a practice, a traditional rule of thumb, and do not have the quality of a Universal Principle.

Free choice, however, does not exempt us from the effect of natural laws. Laws, cultures and political constitutions and rules vary from city to city, from London to Beijing, for example. The fact that fire will burn with the same force in both cities illustrates how a natural principle is uniform, whereas man-made convention is variable.

The difference between a beehive and the human city is that one is entirely the creation of human nature. Wherever bees form a hive it is the same, determined by their instinct, whereas the human city involves more than this. Human choice develops different politics for different places, different governments and laws. Wherever rules or procedures are not in harmony with underlying principles or causes, the corresponding effect or consequence will be disharmony. Natural laws are not discerning, they operate regardless of our awareness of them or obedience to them. The ignorance of a law cannot excuse us from a law in which principles are emphatic.

Principles are not invented by us, as practices are, and they apply in all situations, whatever the circumstances. Often, when experiencing a difficulty, we look for security in a practice, a prescribed way of dealing with something that has worked in a previous situation. But when the practice does not work with the current situation we experience feelings of incompetence. When we understand and live our lives based on principles, we will be able to apply them in any circumstances. Understanding a practice helps us meet the current problem sufficiently, but understanding the principle behind the practices empowers us to meet future challenges actively.

Teaching our children practices which were suitable for our own circumstances may not prepare them for the challenges they will meet in their lives. Children, and for that matter, new colleagues and employees, seem to have a natural built-in 'test it' sensor which asks 'why' when being shown a particular way of doing something. These occasions should be used as an opportunity to test the practice, to see if there is an underlying principle which allows it to work in different circumstances. They are opportunities to establish how effective the practice is and whether it can be improved. The principle of asking questions develops understanding and empowerment, but what is achieved by doing something in a certain way simply because that is how it has always been done? Certainly not innovation and creativity. When someone next asks you why something is done in a particular way, be aware how you respond. Do you react with annoyance when the practice is questioned? Do you interpret it as a slight on your position? Does it make you feel less secure in your position? Would you reply by explaining the principle underlying the practice?

The following 2,500-year-old advice from the East subtly sums up the difference between principle and practice: 'Give someone a fish and you feed them for a day, teach them how to fish and you feed them for a lifetime.'

Cause and Effect

One single principle brings together all the great wisdom and literature of over 6 thousand years. Sages and deep thinkers in all civilizations and religions have discussed its immutable factors and the paradoxes and puzzles that flow from it. This principle is that of cause and effect, where cause is the principle and the effect is the vibratory pattern or process that emerges from it.

In the East this principle is referred to as the way for life. It's a principle meaning how – how things happen and work. Whatever is thought or done in life emerges from the underlying principles of 'oneness'. If a thought or deed is not in harmony with this, the resulting vibratory pattern or process will be correspondingly turbulent. Everything in the universe is related and therefore subject to the same laws.

The Interaction of Opposites

Creation consists of things and events which are all vibratory. Vibration consists of polarities and opposites which may co-operate or conflict with one another to varying degrees. Regardless of whether they are co-operative or conflicting, harmonious or turbulent, all things and events manifest themselves in accordance with the cause or principle. With a knowledge of how polarities work, the wise individual and leader learns not to push in order to make things happen, but to allow the process to evolve on its own. If you let go of the result, leaving it to the process, and are aware of your thoughts and actions, the results will take care of themselves.

With principles, what is seemingly paradoxical is actually logical: listening before speaking, coiling before springing, starting at the beginning, and sowing before reaping. Yet the results springing from the process are what is wanted. All behaviours contain their opposites: a show of strength suggests insecurity, if you want to prosper be generous, hyper-inflation leads to collapse. The paradox of adhering to principles works – you have to let go in order to achieve. For example, when you give up trying to impress the group, you become very impressive. When you just try to make yourself look good, the group knows that and does not like it.

The best work is done when you forget your own point of view: the less you make of yourself, the more you are.

In yielding to the wishes of the person working with you, you encounter no resistance. In the same way that water wears away rock and spirit overcomes force, learn to see things in a different way, from the inside out.

Have you ever struggled to get love, work or a deal and finally given up only to find love, work or a deal suddenly there? Too much force always backfires. Constant intervention and instigation disturb the process. Driven by efficiency the leaders who push are not facilitating process but are in fact effectively blocking it. Leaders can often think that their position gives them absolute authority and that their constant interventions are a measure of their ability. The fact is that their behaviours diminish respect and the interventions are an impediment and inappropriate. The true leader teaches by example rather than by lecturing others on how they ought to be.

Being oneself is acting in harmony with the principle of oneness, and is far more potent than creating an impression. Style is no substitute for substance and the individual who is true to him- or herself is more down to earth and can do what needs doing more effectively than the person who is merely busy.

Whatever emerges from a principle or cause needs to be nurtured by virtue. As behaviour consists of opposites, trying too hard can produce unexpected results. If anything is done to excess its polarity will appear: striving to be beautiful makes a person ugly and trying too hard to be kind is a form of selfishness. Flashy leaders lack stability (trying to appear brilliant is not enlightened), and insecure leaders try to promote themselves. All these behaviours come from insecurity and in turn they feed insecurity.

The Three Principal Virtues

Virtues nurture the process of an action. Temperance prevents excess of a direction, Courage maintains direction, Justice ensures the direction is correct. These three principal virtues develop towards an ultimate good – happiness. Virtues are precepts to happiness as means to an end. Additional virtues, such as prudence or practical wisdom, and intuitive reason or understanding, are developed from living by these principal three.

From all these fundamental virtues emerge the values of integrity, fairness, compassion, industry, sincerity, discipline and order. These values are aligned to Universal Principles and are the ingredients for developing excellence of character and mind in depth and substance. The Universal Principle that says you will receive the corresponding effect for your actions can work with you or against you. For example, to the degree that you are not yourself you will cease to be yourself, and will feel the internal turmoil accordingly. The degree of quality, sustainability and happiness you receive from the goals you set in your life, tangible and intangible, will be in direct proportion to how much the underlying values are aligned to principles.

Influencing Others

All growth spreads outward from a fertile potent nucleus. You are your own nucleus and anything you do will cause a ripple effect. Do you want to be a positive influence in the world? Then first get your own life in order. Ground yourself in the simple principle that your thinking is wholesome and effective. If you do that, you will earn respect and be a powerful influence. In turn, your behaviour will influence others through the ripple effect, because everyone influences everyone else. Powerful people are powerful influences. If your life works, you influence your family and colleagues. If your families and teams work, they influence their community and organization. Influences begin with you and ripple outwards, so be sure that your influence is both potent and wholesome. When you practise a way of life and demonstrate co-operation with this principle, you will experience the power of universal harmony.

Developing personally and professionally develops your character and competence. You feel more secure in yourself and are able to see things in a different light. Life is an opportunity, not an obligation; and effective leaders motivate people to the highest levels by offering opportunities, not obligations. Effective managers do not achieve production through constraint and limitation, but by providing opportunities.

Understanding Universal Principles means understanding how things happen. But how things happen is not the same as 'what should I do?' No one can tell you what to do. That is your freedom. That is your responsibility. Instead of asking for advice, learn to become more conscious of what is actually happening. Then you will be able to see for yourself how things happen. You can make your own decisions about what to do. Whatever you do is your own responsibility. But the pattern of your behaviour follows a natural law. This law is so general it covers every possible event, and so specific it applies to every instance of every event. Another should not decide for you what to do in a given situation. That is up to you. Being responsible for your own actions is a fundamental principle for building character. Allowing others to be responsible for your actions is a practice which cannot develop this skill.

Detecting Principles

Principles are not values. We know that the frame of reference in our head dictates our expectations and the subsequent direction they usually take in our life. This value system determines how we progress. We have seen that having the correct map will have a much more dramatic effect than simply developing our attitudes and behaviours. But the essential tool which makes any map effective is the compass that aligns it. This always acts on the same north principle, regardless of the map.

Maps are only effective when aligned with true north, and values are only effective when aligned with principles. Our built-in conscience acts as our compass, and being aware of it allows us to detect principles easily. In any serious study of families or organizations the reality of such principles becomes obvious. We may argue the definition of principles, their inter-pretations and applications, but in real-life situations there is general agreement about their intrinsic worth. And when our values are developed in line with them, we can enjoy harmony and balance in all areas of life.

The reason for understanding how principles and mindsets work is to ensure the development of a strong foundation for what you plan to achieve in your life and business. Although planning is invaluable, plans themselves can become worthless within months. But when there is commitment to a set of principles, the individual planning goals or actions has a direc-tional compass applicable to every set of circumstances that the plan may meet.

The usual practice in business and life is to set goals or objectives, establish a plan of action and then enjoy the reward. This paradigm lacks substance and often the attainment of a goal does not turn out as it was originally intended. As obstacles are met we push harder, often employing quick-fix solutions in order not to delay the achievement of our goals. As a result we may feel empty and exhausted when the goal is reached. In addition, the rewards or satisfaction received on attaining the goal are often unsustainable, and not as important as was originally thought.

A more thorough paradigm is required if we are to establish the kind of foundation conducive to effective consequences and results which will be sustainable in the long term. The diagrams that follow (pages 34 and 35) illustrate two processes: the Societal Practised Paradigm and the Balanced Holistic Paradigm Alternative.

The Societal Paradigm illustrates a process which has proved to be highly successful in the short term. It is the important long-term situation which is strenuous. No one is really interested in getting what they crave. We are really interested in being at peace with ourselves but our conditioning has prevented us from knowing how to go about this.

We live in two worlds, an inner and an outer world. The outer world has an external influence on us. We see our homes, finances, jobs, cars and other people as our security. Our internal world of thoughts, feelings and desires, our insight and curiosity, has the ability to motivate us internally. We must place our internal world first because quite simply it controls and determines the outer world. Common sense such as this has been recorded in every true religion and philosophy, but while giving it lip-service mankind chooses to perform a different yet common practice.

Your security is not to be found in what you do or what you call yourself – it is in what you are.

The Holistic Paradigm illustrates a process which has been proved to make an individual at home in both the internal and

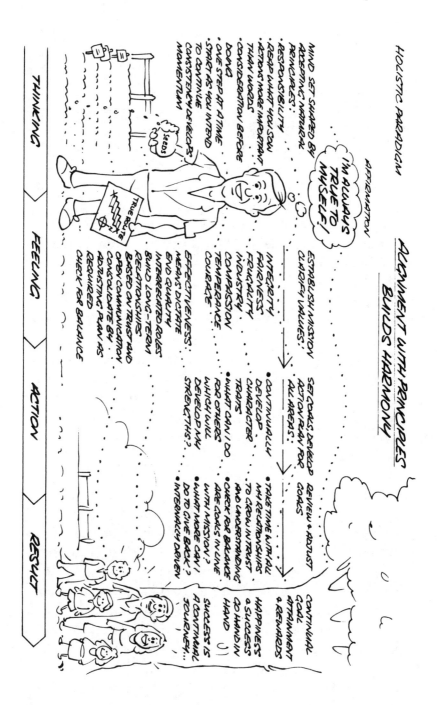

external worlds because, although living in them both simultaneously, the inner world is always placed first. Any actions are a result of thinking that has its values rooted in Universal Laws.

Society mindsets produce assumptions which spring from fixed thinking and produce the same picture, although perhaps in a different frame. We must guard ourselves against seeing what we merely wish to see. If people under stage hypnosis see lions chasing them, do you get them to run faster, give them guns, or wake up their thinking?

If we allow ourselves to be hypnotized by false illusions we will continue to restrict our ability to grow in a truly meaningful way. Our chief illusion, and one which breeds all others, is a false sense of self. So long as we regard ourselves as being other than what we are, we will never be able to develop the full trust and communication necessary for developing what we really want out of our life – genuine peace of mind. Yet by letting go of false illusions through increased awareness we can become true to ourselves. When we achieve this we are in harmony with Universal Principles. We become our own principle, our own cause, and all processes coming from our actions will be conducive to continuous improvement in our lives.

Creating Balance

The classic line from Lao Tzu's *Tao Te Ching*, 'A journey of a thousand miles begins with a single step', is analogous to the process of developing character, relationships and achievements. They all follow the principle of one step at a time: understanding basic language comes before advanced language; walls are not built after the roof. You can learn to do 30 press-ups by building them up over a period of time, say 30, 60 or 90 days, but you cannot do 30 immediately, you have to develop the capacity first. Too often, however, people develop crisis in their lives by taking a short cut. When a step is missed or jumped over without consolidation, the resultant effect on balance is strenuously felt, perhaps not in the short term but certainly in the long term. Most people reading this will be acutely aware of this fact, but many do not apply the wisdom. To know and not to act is not to understand its importance. The common rationalization is: 'Yes, that's all very well and makes good sense, but the reality is that there isn't time. The real world is dog eat dog. I need the money. I need that deal.' Is the reality the first illusion we have about ourselves? Doing whatever it takes means doing what is important and not attending to what is urgent. And doing what is important is the only basis for obtaining sustainable results.

Regardless of home or business, a successful outcome depends on successful interaction with other people. People will only do repeat business with people they know, like and trust. The basis of a long-term relationship is trust and you have to take the 'know' and 'like' steps first – you cannot jump straight to 'trust'. Trust itself can only follow the steps of individual trustworthiness. How is trustworthiness developed? Through development of its fundamental components: character and competence. Only through truthfulness and integrity – the ability to make and keep promises to yourself – can this be developed properly. In turn the value of integrity comes from the principle of being true to yourself.

ALIGNMENT CREATES BALANCE

CAUSE: EFFECT:

UNIFYING PRINCIPLES ———→ SPIRITUAL ←——— MEANINGFUL VALUES

ESTABLISHED MISSION ———→ MENTAL ←——— SENSE OF BELONGING

WORTHWHILE GOALS ———→ EMOTIONAL ←——— QUALITY OF LIFE

ACTION PLANS ———→ PHYSICAL ←——— QUALITY OF RESULTS

NON-ALIGNMENT CREATES IMBALANCE

CAUSE: EFFECT:

— ———————→ SPIRITUAL ←——— VALUES?

NO MISSION ———→ MENTAL ←——— SENSE OF LONGING

DESIRED GOALS' ———→ EMOTIONAL ←——— QUALITY OF LIFE

ACTION PLANS ———→ PHYSICAL ←——— QUALITY OF RESULTS

Balance Leads to Unity

There is an old story about a community of eagles that lived on a beautiful mountain range. They were carefree and happy, finding an abundance of natural foods in the surrounding woods and streams, and their days were spent in lofty soaring and peaceful pleasure.

But down on the dry prairie there dwelled a band of clever crows. Merchants by occupation, the crows had invested their money in growing a low grade of corn. In their search for potential customers they noticed the eagles flying high in the distance. 'Why don't we sell them the corn?' they said to each other, and made a committee to discuss how they could persuade the birds to buy it.

'You must develop a nice glittering package to put the corn in,' said one crow. 'It is important to get the eagles dependent on us,' suggested another. 'And most important of all,' said a third who had had considerable success in selling corn, 'We must convince the eagles that our corn is not merely a need but that it is an absolute must. We must persuade them that without it they will be lonely, loveless and lost. And a good starting place is to load them with a false sense of guilt. Just make them feel guilty about ignoring our corn and we've got them!'

Now the eagles were quite intelligent but somewhat careless in their thinking. Although they were cautious and suspicious at first, the corn looked pretty good, and it saved them the effort of actually going out and hunting for it themselves. So the eagles soared less and less and dropped down to the cornfields more and more. Of course, the less they flew, the less they felt like flying. As their wings grew weak they had to hop awkwardly over the ground. This led to frequent collisions with each other, followed by quarrels and arguments.

But there was one eagle whose eyesight also gave him

insight. He sensed something very wrong about the whole operation. Besides, the corn just did not taste right. When he tried to persuade his friends to return to the mountains, the crows ridiculed him as a trouble-maker. And for causing trouble with the crows, the eagles shunned their former friend.

So the more corn the crows peddled, the more corn the eagles swallowed. But something had now happened to the once lovely kings of birds. They complained a lot. They were nervous and irritable. They felt lonely, loveless and lost. Every once in a while they would remember their mountain home, but could not remember the way back. So they sullenly existed, hoping something better would turn up, which it never did.

Meanwhile, the keen-eyed eagle had grown tired of it all, and studied himself carefully. Rediscovering his wings, he tried them out. They worked! So off he flew back to the mountains, and from dawn to sunset he soared once again over his world, carefree and happy.

And this is how each of us, tired of it all, can fly up and away to find our natural freedom and happiness. The first thing we have to do is change our thinking in order to release ourselves from our conditioning. There is a mental faculty above and beyond the conditioned human thought – our true mind. It is the same as awareness or consciousness. It is what an Eastern mystic would call the Silent Mind, or what the New Testament calls the Kingdom of Heaven Within. It is your true self. Quite simply, it is the force within every man and woman that is as high above the conditioned mind as the sky is above the earth. The true mind is free of all negative conditions. It has no fear, no painful cravings, no doubts. It knows everything necessary for a successful and happy life.

The conditioned mind is that part of us which has been influenced and moulded since birth. It is an acquired mass of opinions, beliefs, contradictions and mechanical reactions, all of which get us into trouble. As the conditioned mind does not represent our basic self, everyone can and must break away from it.

Being true to yourself is the fundamental principle that applies in all facets of life. It is the very essence of self-unity from which true happiness comes. Without self-unity it would be unimportant what choices we made in life; as long as they are based on fleeting desires or egotistical ambitions, no good can occur. If we are not true to ourselves we will never attain true satisfaction, only an empty thrill. When whatever we decide is from the centre of our consciousness, authentic gains can be made.

The dissatisfaction of most people is never a sharp stab, but a dull ache. It doesn't bite, it gnaws – a gnawing belief that others are happier than they are. Many seek happiness in future events, mentally matching the outcome with their desires. And when the outcomes are not as hoped for, frustration is certain. Happiness cannot be known in advance. The attraction of new surroundings, success in an enterprise or winning something soon fades, leaving us as empty as we were before. We are no different or any happier. Happiness reveals itself from moment to moment. It cannot be forecast because it follows natural laws.

Our conditioned or unnatural thinking is the cause of unnatural conditions. Natural satisfaction is the effect of natural thinking. True happiness lies in what actually happens to us, not in what we prophesy should happen. Fifteen hundred years ago the Roman philosopher Boethius wrote in his work *The Consolation of Philosophy*: 'The perfect and abiding source of happiness is possession of the true self.'

Next time you feel unhappy don't label yourself as unhappy, instead see yourself as confused about things. This sets in motion an entirely different process – a healthy one. By thinking you are unhappy you create the feeling of unhappiness. Marcus Aurelius said: 'It is not the event that controls you, it is your estimate of the event.' By changing your thinking you can look to solve the situation by studying the underlying principle. In this way you can develop self-unity. Accept that it is your fixed ideas that are creating the situation that causes unhappiness.

Through self-awareness and self-evaluation you can break through conditioned ways of thinking and return to a stronger natural mindset. True happiness and satisfaction can then be experienced under all circumstances. You become true to yourself and experience Universal Principles working for you rather than against you. A river always gets where it is going; any obstacle it meets it does not take personally, it simply overcomes it. The water's strength, persistence and resilience is in its unity. Like the river you become more fluid and less rigid with self-unity.

The old Indian parable of two birds in a tree illustrates our insecurity. One, on an upper branch, sits in quiet and peaceful contemplation of all that goes on around him. The other hops nervously from one branch to another to sample the fruit. Coming across sweet fruit he chirps excitedly, tasting sour fruit he falls into disgust and depression. Glancing up from time to time he is vaguely impressed by the magnificent manner of the bird above. The nervous bird longs to know the secret of the serenity of the other, but soon forgets his yearning when the sight of new fruit attracts his attention.

So back and forth, up and down he hops, switching every few minutes from sweet fruit to sour, from elation to disappointment, from smiles to tears. Seeking only sweet fruit, he despairingly realizes that the sweet is always followed by the bitter. No matter what he does, sour follows sweet. He glances hopefully upwards at the peaceful bird, but compulsively returns to his frantic searchings. The time comes however when he gets a mouthful of fruit so bitter that he can hardly bear it. He is at crisis point. He must choose something entirely different or lose his sanity. So he hesitantly hops up towards the peaceful bird, coming closer and closer.

At a certain point in his timid approach, a miracle occurs, the lower bird realizes that he was the upper bird all along! He simply did not see it. In his illusion he thought there were two separate birds, but now knows that only one exists – his unified self.

Now perceiving that his frantic hopping was done in a state of hypnotic illusion, and knowing that he himself is the majestic bird, he is above both excitement and grief. He no longer seeks happiness outside himself – his true self is happiness itself!

Let the moral of this story be a source of strength and comfort to you – you are never without the urge to find the way upward and back to your original self. You have made a major break-through when you realize that beyond your conditioned way of thinking a true-self way of thinking actually exists.

Unifying Principles

The principles discussed here are constant, and regardless of family, company or huge organization, the same principles apply. Many believe that home and work are separate and therefore apply different values to these areas. But duplicity of values creates chaos. Quarrels and tensions experienced at home when trust is low are manifested in departmental criticism and in-house politics. Such negative effects occur when life is conducted without understanding and adhering to Universal Principles.

As you focus on principles you empower everyone who understands those principles to act, without constantly having to monitor, evaluate, correct or control. Principles have universal applications and when these are internalized into habits they enable people to create a wide variety of practices to deal with different situations.

Many individuals in teams and companies are given the same direction, and the practice of 'go along to get along' is dominant. But the same direction does not necessarily mean the same focus, which all too often is lacking. Security is looked for in status, position, hidden agendas, criticism and credit seeking. Alignment of an organization's missions and values is not possible if there is no trust on an interpersonal level. Consequently, empowerment is often tried but soon viewed as a 'programme of the month' as lack of trust brings back control from above.

With no involvement there can be no commitment and any mission statement formulated by a board is not bought into. As a result it simply hangs on a wall in a fancy frame and induces cynicism and disillusionment.

The above scenario is not an attractive one but this environment exists in many major organizations. Only through a change in thinking can an atmosphere be changed. Systems and strategies can be tried and quality management brought in.

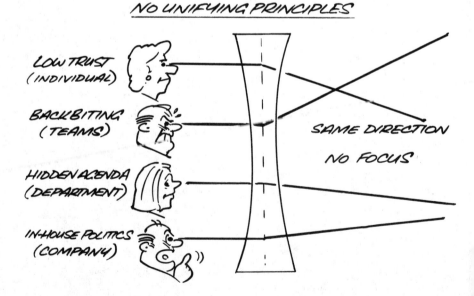

All is pointless short-termism unless the approach is one of developing the individual from the inside out. The human resource paradigm of developing the individual does not go far enough. It needs to be transcended by an alternative that begins with generating an understanding and belief of these unifying principles. It is these which govern the strength of an organization.

Through development of trustworthiness at individual level and an alignment of personal missions and values with those of the organization, key individuals can then in turn influence the wider teams and departments by their example. The 'them and us' attitude will diminish as the source of the attitude and behaviour is changed to embrace the fact that security is not in 'one of them' or 'one of us'. It is rooted in individuals' firm belief that they are responsible for their actions and their influence on others. The individual who receives the problem owns the problem and this will be the norm.

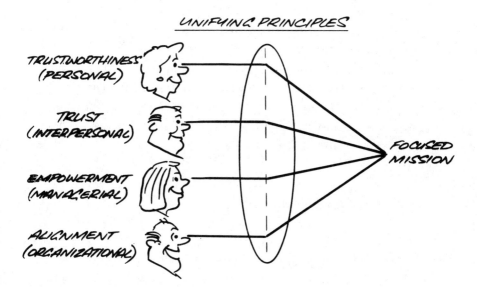

Systems and practices can be constantly reviewed by anyone who chooses to ask 'why do we do it this way?' As the system producers improve, so will the systems. Genuine pride will be felt as missions are focused within the broadening horizons. Open lines of communication will create deeper lines of empathy between groups, which in turn will develop as a result of increased synergy.

This type of alternative management thinking will provide you as an individual with a new freedom to be true to yourself while making a more effective contribution to your business and your team. It will help you to develop a natural thinking in harmony with the Universal Laws, which will work for you and not against you. It will release every ounce of potential within whole companies and alleviate the traditional chaos that results from volatile and rapidly changing environments.

New thinking will create new rules and new opportunities, which before had been either overlooked or unrecognizable. The dramatic increase in innovation and creativity will be in direct proportion to the reduction in the barriers to trust and communication. The 'Aha!' feeling will be felt far more frequently. This more balanced environment, based on the principles at the centre of our lives, will induce the Eureka Effect.

Although it is our nature to compartmentalize, define and measure everything we come across, Universal Laws cannot be as specifically treated as man-made laws. However, for reference, the fundamental laws which control the quality of our lives can be summarized as follows.

Seven Key Universal Laws

1 *The Law of Cause and Effect*
   This is the fundamental law of life. For everything that happens to you there is a specific cause. Thoughts are causes

and conditions are effects, so whatever thoughts you sow will culminate in an action which will reap the corresponding effect. It is the mental counterpart of the Newtonian Physical law that 'for every action there is an equal and opposite reaction', and it operates on the same principle.

Any form of energy sent out (cause) cannot go to nothing: it has to manifest itself as something (effect). As natural laws are not discerning, it is important to keep your mind on what you want and not on what you don't want. The quality of your relationships, for example, at any given moment will be the result of what you have sown in those relationships. Many other more specific laws come from this law, for example, the Law of Correspondence. This is the New Testament principle of 'as within so without': your outer world is a mirror and reflects what is going on in your inner world.

2 *The Law of Attraction*
Whatever you predominantly think about will attract into your life the people and circumstances which are in harmony with those thoughts. Metaphysically, the greater the vibration you send out (vibration being relative to your concentration), the more powerful the attraction. This is similar to the physical Law of Resonance. When you set off several metronomes at different levels in one room they will soon all beat at the level of the strongest vibration. You will always attract whatever you think about, positive or negative. Common sense therefore tells you what to think about, yet common practice often prevents you.

3 *The Law of Creativity*
Out of two interactive energies, yin and yang, male and female, comes a third. There is an infinite supply of ideas available to you to tune into, and all of them will dramatically develop your potential, your happiness and your success. To the degree that you become true to yourself, your

ability to harness your own interactive energies increases and you are able to tune into these insights and inspirations. (See the sixth chapter for more details.)

4   *The Law of Substitution*
You cannot simply stop doing something. Holding a void or vacuum is not sustainable by any amount of willpower or determination. To stop a habit or attitude you must substitute another for it. Your conscious mind, for example, can only hold one thought at a time, positive or negative. Replace the thought of what you don't want to happen with the thought of what you do want to happen. Something cannot go to nothing: it has to be replaced or re-channelled by substitution.

5   *The Law of Service*
Do not serve others in a way you would not wish to be served yourself, for your return will always equal your service. Treat the person behind the desk in the way that you would treat the person in front of the desk, as the return operates on the same principle. You will always be rewarded in life in exact proportion to the value of your service to others. The 'I' is developed through the 'we'.

6   *The Law of Use*
Any natural strength, gift or talent will atrophy if it is not used, and become stronger in direct proportion to how much it is used. This is well illustrated by the story of the old man who showed Rossetti, the famous painter, the drawings he had recently done in his retirement. Rossetti replied politely that they were only mediocre. The old man then showed some other drawings which had obviously been done by a younger man and which Rossetti immediately praised, saying that here was indeed some great talent and that with training and practice the individual could become a great painter. On seeing the old man overcome with emotion he enquired if it

was perhaps the man's son. The man replied: 'No, they are the drawings I did as a young man. But I was persuaded to do something else.' The old man's gift had disappeared. Use it or lose it.

7 *The Law of Seven*

A succession of events proceeds according to the Law of Seven or the law of octaves. As the notes of a scale are played, each note resounds for a certain time and then diminishes in intensity. The Law of Seven means that no force ever works continuously in the same direction. It works for a certain time, then diminishes in intensity and either changes its direction or undergoes an inner change.

No process in the world goes without interruption. The key lies in knowing how to accept interruptions and obstacles and in being aware when to start the next 'octave'. If we push too much in one direction, what we want goes further away. If we are internally motivated and continually seek improvement, the interruptions will be seen as what they are, part of the growing process. It is the process of what we do which is important, not the result – after all, we have no control over the result. In the same way, we have control over choice but not over consequence.

Nothing in nature develops in a straight line and neither does your life, but to the extent that you align yourself with these principles you flow with their tide not against it. The Law of Seven shows that no force can develop in one direction only and that energy develops even amongst the obstacles and intervals. Full understanding of the Law of Seven, which is beyond the scope of this book, leads to the understanding of the Seven Levels of Consciousness. Similar to octaves, everything in life goes by vibrations. No vibration, no movement and therefore no activity can go on in any other way.

THIRD: A Sense of ...

OBSERVATION

If it is Universal Principles that create harmony and quality of life, how can we be certain to align our values to them? Quite simply, through our conscience. Our most significant world is our inner world. In that world is self-awareness, independent will, creative imagination and conscience. Through self-evaluation we are able to look clearly to our paradigms, beliefs and motives. The process of self-awareness develops our awareness of our conscience, how it works and how it can be used to create and develop a balanced life.

Conscience and Morality

It is important to differentiate between morality and conscience. Morality is not constant. It is different between countries, centuries, decades, classes, people of different education and so on. What may be moral in one culture may be immoral in another.

Morality is always different and it always changes, but conscience never changes. Conscience is a kind of emotional understanding of truth in certain different relations, generally in relations to behaviour and actions and to people. This is always the same and cannot change; it cannot differ from one nation to another, from one country to another, or from one person to another. Where morality is relative, conscience is absolute.

Conscience, however, does help us to be aware of what is good and bad about our conduct. Conscience is a state in which we cannot hide anything of our conduct, and its development, which is necessary for growth and substance, is parallel and simultaneous with the development of our consciousness and self-awareness. Conscience is related to emotions in the same way that consciousness is related to ideas. To have a moment of conscience is to experience at once all our feelings about somebody or something. Most people do not use their conscience to its full potential so that when it does arise it always brings uncomfortable feelings – even suffering – for it is very unpleasant to face the truth about ourselves.

As all the feelings relating to somebody and something are expressed in a moment of conscience, whether we like it or not, we have many methods of dealing with this to prevent ourselves feeling uncomfortable. Such methods include imagination, negative emotions and, in particular, justification. Conscience can be defined as an emotional feeling of truth on a given subject. Where consciousness is the 'intellectual' part of self-awareness, conscience is the 'emotional' part.

Conscience is the part of our consciousness that is vital to our self-development and awareness.

If its current format always makes us feel uncomfortable and if it 'turns' against us whenever it manifests itself, then it must be awakened in order that we can release its force for our individual growth.

Quite simply, if we do not have a definite aim, and do not work for a certain definite purpose, the function of the conscience is only to spoil life for those who are unlucky enough to have it. But if we work for a definite purpose, conscience helps us to attain our aim. Without understanding and development of our conscience the natural conscience of what is right and what is wrong will continue to lie dormant behind the conditioned conscience of 'Will I be found out?' Our natural conscience is a special positive emotion, whereas our conditioned conscience becomes caught up in the exchange of negative energy. When-ever you seek to defend or justify yourself, or return the same treatment because 'they did it to you', you are working from the outside in with self-defeating negative emotion.

Developing Conscience

By developing your conscience as an ally and trusted advisor rather than an irritating acquaintance you have to tolerate, you will develop the insight of an internal compass. This will ensure that your internal map aligns your external actions to natural principles. Conscience in conditioned life is no more than association. We are accustomed to think and do things in a certain way and if for some reason we act in a different way we have an unpleasant feeling which we call conscience. When developed to its stronger and deeper state it becomes a definite method of cognition, a useful tool for discrimination. We are able to recognize the quality inherent in principles and verify other things by these principles.

Developing conscience means breaking down the internal 'walls' that prevent us from facing our inner contradictions and seeing the truth about ourselves. These walls divide us into thought-proof compartments. We compartmentalize what is effectively the same emotional feeling about something. We create contradictory desires, intentions and aims from moment to moment, but we do not see that they are contradictions because these walls prevent us looking from one compartment to another. At one moment we feel one thing and at another something quite different. If we could feel all the feelings that we have about something we would awaken our true conscious-ness. That would be conscience. Throughout life our habitual ways of thinking have only one aim – to avoid unpleasant feelings and realizations about ourselves. People never really see how contradictory they are with themselves. If they did they would be unable to trust themselves.

Developed conscience can have a bird's eye view of all our different compartments and show us how we think and feel about one thing, then another thing and then again quite a different thing, all on the same subject. Opinions, prejudices and preconceived ideas are solid walls. If people have a con-stant wrong attitude based on wrong information, are self- or work-centred rather than principle-centred, they always use the same kind of excuse. In doing so they build those walls which become permanent. In this way people develop fixed ideas and complete misconceptions about themselves.

People can believe, for example, that they are always on time, yet actually they are consistently late. When their atten-tion is drawn to this they are astonished and reply, 'Well, I may not always be punctual but I am never late.' Wrong assumptions and misconceptions about ourselves, our capacity, our powers, inclinations and awareness often take the form of a strong conviction. I remember one person who was convinced he was a nice person who liked simply everyone. In reality he liked no one, but his strong 'self-convinced' conviction made him free to be as unpleasant and rude as he liked. Walls are built up by education and surroundings, but the strongest are created by self-education. A classic situation involves people whose posi-tion has led them to believe that they are excellent judges of character, and that they are able to evaluate someone quickly. Yet these people have never evaluated themselves using the same criteria.

Before you are qualified to evaluate another, you need to have evaluated yourself.

Over the years I have asked many, many managers, leaders, and people in positions of responsibility if they have to evaluate other people on a regular basis. The answer is, of course, always yes. On a daily basis their positions involve the constant evaluation of colleagues, subordinates, teams, departments, clients and customers. I then ask them if they have seriously and consistently evaluated themselves on a daily basis. Only five per cent were able to answer yes.

The third question I ask is delivered on the basis that they answer from what their conscience and heart say and not from

what their intellect and head say. The question is: 'Do you think that before you are qualified to evaluate another or be a character judge, you need to have evaluated yourself regarding your own thoughts and actions?' Not one of them has ever disagreed and, moreover, all admit that true leaders would greatly increase their effectiveness with personnel if this action became habitual. They see that the common practice of not doing this is not common sense. Their not doing it stems from not thinking about it. In order to change their thinking they must increase their self-awareness.

In order to utilize conscience effectively one of the first prerequisites is sincerity with ourselves. We seldom experience this. Can you think of a time? How can you learn to be sincere with yourself? Only by trying to see yourself. Just think about yourself, not in emotional moments, but in quiet moments, and do not justify yourself – generally we justify and explain every-thing by saying that it was inevitable, it was somebody else's fault, and so on. In order to tell the difference between what is happening and what is not happening you have to become aware. This means becoming silent and listening, really listening, to your inner thoughts.

Self-Observation

The definition of awareness itself is very simple. It means that we stand aside and watch everything happening to us, both within and without. Most people 'assume' that they are already self-aware. Everyone thinks this is the case, but awareness must not be assumed, it must be experienced. In your external world start by noticing how people are unaware of their movements. Observe how their extremities fidget: their fingers drum or twiddle a pencil, their feet swing up and down, they gesture while talking. Then start to observe your own physical actions, your movements and your expressions. Notice how you were unaware of them.

Now observe internally. Watch how feelings and irritations arise when someone criticizes or questions you. Notice how you feel when you receive bad news or good news. See how you arouse waves of depression or excitement respectively. In this way you begin to see yourself as you are. To have read about a painting is to know about it, but not actually to see it. Without 'experiencing' the actual picture is your knowledge sufficient to evaluate it? To see it once is not sufficient as different thoughts arrive at different moments. If you look at the picture regularly you may become aware of things that you had not observed before. It is the same with evaluating yourself, you have to see yourself regularly as others see you in order to start seeing and therefore know completely your true self. In this way you can begin to differentiate between your true self and your conditioned false self.

Observe your inner feelings when you are with others in various circumstances. Are you relaxed or uneasy, timid or talkative? Are you compelled to be the life and soul of the party? Do you allow yourself to be carried along or perform in a certain fashion, with or without your consent? Next observe yourself when you are alone. Are you invariably more at ease when by yourself? More relaxed? If the answer is yes, this is what you do.

**Work at being just as relaxed with others
as you are when by yourself.**

Do not allow the mere presence of others to make you nervous. Slowly but surely the cosmetic yet compulsive behaviour you portray with others will disappear. You will not experience the strenuous and often exhausting effect that 'putting on the right face' brings, even though you had previously been unaware of it. You will remain relaxed. There is no barrier to the achievement of your true self. The supposed barrier is only a mirage of wrong thinking.

There is really no such thing as a tense or uncomfortable situation with others. What really bothers you is the behaviour and explanations you falsely think you owe to others. You owe nothing to others except to be real, and they owe nothing but the same to you. Do not expect anything else from anyone, for you alone can give true value to yourself. Learn to notice the difference between the inner feelings you have when talking to someone when wanting something from them and those you have when you do not want something.

Knowledge without understanding is useless, but by observing and studying ourselves we can increase our understanding of why we do things in the way that we do, often to our detriment. All tension results from an individual's attempt to prove that an illusion is a reality. To go further, tension is not caused by human conflict; rather, conflict is caused by human tension. Permanent relaxation comes as we relax our imaginary ideas about ourselves. Tension and exhaustion arise from defending ourselves and our ideas.

Learn to question all your ideas which you feel you must defend, as in this way you are defending your false self. The truth needs no defence, no justification. It can be explained but never needs defending. We have to become aware of an unhappy state before we can get rid of it. Notice your tension when trying to please people from whom you want something – observe it. The tension is created from the mistaken belief that others can give you psychological rewards – consolation or excitement. When you begin to stop thinking in this way all your human relationships will be without tension.

The basic rule about self-evaluation is that the amount of self-understanding can be tested by observing the amount of self-concern. The more insight, the less concern. The less insight, the more concern. In your striving and hard work do you ever feel overwhelmed by the futility of it all? Listen carefully to that feeling, when something within you whispers: 'There is a wrong way to live and a right way to live. The wrong way never works. The right way always works.' Now if life is futile that is a friendly message informing you of the wrong way. See this as the way that doesn't work. Become aware of the wrong way, of futility, without feeling bad about it. Where the education of the conscience aligns our purpose with guiding principles, self-awareness is the ear to the voice of conscience. It helps us to recognize that there are principles independent of us, and to understand the futility of trying to become a law unto ourselves.

Self-awareness empowers us to ask 'Am I allowing the good to take the place of the best?' The best may be the unexpected opportunity, the new knowledge, the new options created by increased understanding. If change is driven primarily by urgency, mood or opposition, it takes us away from the best. If driven by a mission, conscience and principles, it moves us towards the best. To have this self-awareness to know the difference between the good and the best and to act in a manner based on mission, conscience and principles is to make valuable inroads towards professional integrity, which develops strength of character. In this way, through consistent self-observation and evaluation you become conscious of yourself. You are able to listen clearly to the direction your conscience gives you. You start to develop your true self. Your external world mirrors your internal world as you literally 'walk your talk'.

Constant evaluation develops your awareness into a bright light. You see things about yourself in a much clearer way. In starting an early morning journey it is difficult to see your direction, you need artificial light. As the sun rises the natural light provides you with clearer vision. Your confidence grows and you relax – the tension of travelling in the dark eases. Start the habit of keeping a journal where you can write down the various reactions, responses and resistances that you have experienced during the day or week. This is not a diary, this is a self-remembering account of your conscious level of awareness. Comment on your feelings about any rejection you have experienced. We learn from rejection, not from acceptance, in the same way that a missile stays on target when its gyro rejects a wrong course. Risk rejection at every opportunity. This is how you break down the walls that harden your thinking. Start becoming aware that the barriers we put up to defend ourselves against illusory enemies are created by the same rules that keep us from breaking out to be true to ourselves. Start in small ways to risk rejection of your favourite ideas while quietly watching how this affects you. Such observation without comment will break down your barriers.

Self-Evaluation

Think about someone in your life who has really caused you pain. As the days turn into weeks and the weeks turn into months you cannot bring yourself to forgive this person. As the months turn into years you say to yourself that although you might forgive you will not forget, and each time something reminds you of that person the pain is not forgotten, it is more deeply buried. The pain you put yourself through is of your own making and develops a strong barrier to your true self.

Ask yourself: 'Is there any way I can release this feeling of pain or sadness towards this person?' Ask yourself if you have it in your power to resolve the hurt. Listen, really listen to your conscience. If the answer you receive is qualified, for example: 'Yes, but the other person would not understand, would not change, I would be wasting my time,' then go deeper. Ask yourself if you alone are able to resolve the pain and hurt you are feeling inside. Ask yourself if you are torturing yourself. Write down the feelings and the answers you become aware of.

In being true to yourself you must refuse the false satisfaction that you harbour as a result of rejection or insult. At first you will feel empty, but this is the emptiness of a garden cleared of weeds, a fresh plot in which you can plant something fruitful. There is no virtue in suffering pain, hurt or guilt.

True understanding and true conscience will come to us when we cease to 'enjoy' our sufferings. The energy with which we indulge our self-hurt is the same energy we use to hurt others, they go hand in hand like all inner and outer world reflections.

We will always treat others exactly as we treat ourselves, though we are rarely aware of this.

With the voluntary abandonment of 'harboured' feelings, our true conscience is able to speak more clearly to us. And with self-observation and evaluation, our increased awareness is able to hear it more clearly.

Through consistent evaluation you will become more aware of your passing thoughts. View them in the same way as you would view ships passing by on the ocean. It is only when you identify with the ships that you will feel distressed. If you say 'this is my ship' you will worry when it passes from sight. If you say 'I must command that ship' you will arouse the fear that someone else will become its captain. Likewise, by simply watching our passing thoughts, we prevent harmful identification with them. In this way we can prevent worry and concern from attaching to us.

Become acquainted with your thinking by carefully

observing it. Let your mind flow and don't try to control it. Let your thoughts follow one after the other, for example: security, then lunch, then worry, then tomorrow, then comfort, then car, then sex, then yesterday, then violence, then television, then work, then mistakes, then desire, then pain. When negative thoughts pass, just observe them casually, then let them go. A negative idea will disappear unless it is held on to and given non-existent value. No more hold a harmful thought in your mind than you would keep rotting food in the cupboard.

As you progress more confidently with your personal evaluation, you begin to see more clearly that the truth which ends depressions also ends family quarrels. Freedom from self-defeating thoughts is also freedom from actions that are later regretted. In understanding your true nature you begin to understand others more effectively. This not only produces change, but you also become a conduit for change.

You will begin to recognize your strengths and weaknesses in a way that empowers you to focus on your strengths rather than correcting your weaknesses – a common practice. Put weaknesses to their proper use as opportunities to develop character. Recognizing and exposing a self-weakness builds strength and wisdom. When people feel they have been cheated by others, the main reason they feel resentful is that their gullibility has been exposed. But a willingness to learn from their humiliation will remove their gullibility. We must remember that the truth which damages our ego is the same truth which strengthens our character.

A self-truth can disturb or heal us to the same degree. For example, if our self-observation reveals jealousy within us, we may want to deny it. But if we simply face the jealousy and see it as an acquired habit, not as part of our essential self, we weaken its hold on us. Defensiveness denies us the freedom that comes from experiencing life to the full. If you timidly avoid a friend with whom you have quarrelled you will remain nervous.

If you permit a meeting with that friend with no preconceived ideas of what to say or do, then you destroy the fear.

In the same way that an underground stream will come to the surface according to its impurity, or non-purity, so we will see the futility of trying to be right with others before being right with ourselves. Our wisdom or non-wisdom in dealing with others will be exactly the same as our wisdom or non-wisdom in dealing with ourselves. For the next seven days observe what happens to yourself as a result of what you do. Notice that when your concentration wanes, mishaps occur; when you act impulsively, you regret it; notice how your thoughts make you nervous, and that when you speak gently to an angry person it has a calming effect.

If you start with the principle that all can be changed by changing the way you think, you are able to observe how you unknowingly create your current world. When someone does something that disturbs you, ask yourself why you are letting it disturb you – examine yourself. Find out why you permit this person to dictate your emotions, ask why you choose to be disturbed instead of being perceptive. When drinking water you can feel whether it is cool or hot. You can also distinguish between cool and comfortable feelings and hot and disturbing feelings. If you feel hot over an insult to your intelligence, be aware of how your feelings burn you.

Next give up the self-righteous, false pleasure of feeling so indignant. Ask yourself 'what do I listen to all day long?' Is it the voice of social propaganda – what society deems you should or should not do? Is it the voice of your own internal distress which forces you to be controlled by external influences? The only true voice is that of your own unified mind.

A mind that attains unity through its own examination, using the true power of conscience, self-awareness and creative imagination, is the only voice of authority. Commence the practice of explaining yourself to yourself, not to others. Use all your experiences with others to develop self-insights. Through constant daily practice of observing your effect on others you will learn how you can correct the actual causes which stem from your current thinking. To learn to think in a new way you must learn to listen to yourself with originality and freshness. Start investing 1 per cent of your day in thoroughly understanding the thoughts and feelings of your interior world. This 14 minutes of investment will reap dividends for the other 99 per cent. Self-insight will develop insight and understanding of others. One flash of insight can clear up a thousand difficulties.

Self-Trust

Most organizations are run according to the mechanical process of managing, directing and controlling, as appropriate. The word organization is derived from 'organic'. To grow something naturally requires the development of leadership attributes at every level of the organization, company or family. A directing manager's security too often becomes part and parcel of position and control. An enhanced 'label' gives greater perceived security, it strengthens a false illusion. Supervising managers often have more rigid thinking than assistant managers; their labels tell them that someone in this position is 'not always right, but never wrong'. When the security of that position is threatened, more control is exerted. Empowerment does not work because a limit is placed on how far people can develop.

If the paradigm of interviewing people were on the basis that they would develop to do a better job than you, can you imagine the potential of true empowerment? Our mindset is that we do not want to make ourselves obsolete so our refrain is 'I taught them all they know' rather than 'I taught them everything I know'. When others start to excel it can threaten our security. Why? Because we allow it to. We seek reasons and

excuses to justify their growth. But you cannot give empowerment to others, each person has to earn it for it to be true
empowerment. Empowerment comes from trust, and self-trust
comes from understanding yourself through evaluation. Self-
knowing individuals can do something that millions of other
people can only yearn to do – they can trust themselves.

Many might believe they live in self-trust when in fact they
live in dependency. They depend on family or career for feelings of security, but fearfully sense their possible loss. These
people have an inner nature that consists of dozens of 'selves'
which constantly compete with each other to become dominant for a few minutes at a time. One minute they are excited,
the next dejected. One part of them is a danger to the other
part. What part can be trusted? None. In self-trust there is no
you and something else which is trusted, there is only a single
state of trust. This develops with the insight that you are really
one with yourself.

The Universal Law in understanding yourself is that each
time you consent to a loss you make a gain. Lose the mood to
appear impressive and important and you no longer bend under
the burden of artificial behaviour. Don't look for security outside yourself and external fluctuations will have no effect on
you. Our external world is what it is because we spend almost
every moment of our lives trying to cover up our insecurities
instead of understanding and dissolving them.

If you feel you need to dominate or control people in order
to gain their respect, they will actually be in control of you and
treat you accordingly. Why? Because anyone from whom you
want something, psychologically speaking, is always in secret
command of you. Any action you take to appear strong before
another is actually read as a weakness. The more you demand
or crave the respect of others, the less likely you are to receive
it. Just think of examples of this behaviour in your own
relationships, particularly with children.

It makes no sense to try to change the way others treat you by learning calculated behaviours or attitude techniques in order to appear in charge. These cosmetics only produce another source of secret inner conflict, which in turn is detrimental to our personal and business relationships. What you are really looking for in your relationships isn't command over others – but over yourself. Trying to impress another, looking for approval, hanging on to every word, expressing contrived concern for well-being, fishing for a kind word, explaining yourself to others, are all examples where you may be sabotaging yourself while assuming you are strengthening your position with others.

Your increasing awareness will notice the building pressure in you when you are doing 'externally influenced' actions. Evaluation as to why you feel the pressure will determine that it is some form of fear and not you wanting to impress or explain. This in itself starts building up the natural feeling of being true to yourself. In any and every given moment of your life you are either in control of yourself or being controlled. Behave the way you really are, even if it ends a relationship. Never suppress yourself in an effort to influence, hold or win someone. When we are unreal, so are rewards. In other words, never behave in the way you think the other person wants you to behave, but in the manner you must.

People are not what they seem. There is as much difference between their exterior and interior states as there is between exterior and interior walls of a house. How can we see people as they are, not as we want or need to see them, in order to evaluate them without mistakes? This can be accomplished by understanding ourselves. When you frankly face your own motives, you see the motives of others.

By understanding your own desires and actions, you understand why others act as they do. Self-knowledge is the key to insight into others. Perhaps in a moment of intense self-honesty a man may see in himself a selfish motive masquerading as generosity. Not only will this realization make him healthier and happier than before, but others can no longer use the same masquerade on him. It works both ways. You understand other people as you understand yourself.

As you gain insight into your own actions the behaviour of others becomes clear.

For every natural strength we have hundreds of weaknesses. In evaluating yourself and observing your natural inclinations and yearnings you become aware of your natural strengths. You are then able to recognize other people's strengths. False illusions about ourselves and conditioned thinking make us dwell on what we are not good at but feel we should be. In turn this makes us look for weaknesses in others. Personnel and human resource managers regularly have to make assessments on many individuals. Although all those individuals' good points are detailed, the assessors' attention is always drawn towards the evaluated weak points. This process is designed to point out weaknesses rather than build on strengths.

Know Your Strengths

When at school I was excellent at history; studying it was a sheer pleasure. Maths, on the other hand, I was hopeless at. I had to work twice as hard to understand half as much. I was advised to put all my energies into maths, my weakest subject, in the belief that my strength (history) would take care of itself. The thinking behind this is that it develops 'good all-rounders'. In my case I failed maths and barely passed history. The practice of fixing weaknesses to make an individual – or for that matter a family, company or organization – stronger and better does not work.

It is a practice that creates mediocrity and is certainly not aligned to the principles that ensure excellence. It is a practice based on the belief that if you can identify all the weaknesses in an individual, team or company, you can dissolve them by developing them into strengths. The practice also believes that existing strengths will take care of themselves so that in the end we will have people who are strong in all the areas we require them to be. If someone is a natural in history, then the area for greatest potential and improvement will be in history. But if he or she is weak in another subject, the emphasis is put on the weak one.

The principle is very clear. Find out what you are good at and do more of it. Find out what you are not good at and don't do it. In sending managers with no interest in selling on sales courses, and salespeople with no interest in administration on admin courses, we believe we are creating efficiency. Yet

effectively we might as well teach pigs to sing. It wastes our time and annoys the pig.

Every day, however, managers evaluate and home in on mistakes, spending time with their weakest performers. Because they believe that the top performers will take care of themselves, the 20 per cent of their time they do spend with them is usually spent demotivating them by pointing out where they are going wrong. Why? Because the whole paradigm of evaluation is to eliminate weaknesses, not simply manage them.

The paradigm is rooted in the belief that weakness is the opposite of strength, as illness is to health, failure to success. Wrong. They are not. Each factor has its own pattern of behaviour and follows its own particular configuration. Thus, studying a weakness will not lead to understanding a strength. In Britain we seek to understand what makes a family stay together by studying what makes a family break up. Similarly, an insurance company that wanted to reduce attrition once asked me to investigate why people were leaving. My suggestion that we find out why people stayed, and then do more of it, was initially rejected as it did not fit the paradigm of 'normal practice'. The commonsense alternative was finally accepted, and the results more than satisfied the initial brief.

The philosophy of the Chinese is that if you develop your strengths to the full, your weaknesses become unimportant. Their constant success at table tennis illustrates this. It is no secret that their weak stroke is the backhand – so they don't use it. Every hour of the day is spent practising the forehand, which develops such invincibility that it cannot be beaten.

Just for a moment think about your greatest mistake or failure. OK, got it? Now think of your greatest success or achievement. Harder, isn't it? Why? Our whole mindset is programmed to root out weaknesses in ourselves and others. We get so good we can spot the weaknesses in someone's presentation or suggestion immediately. We should do, we have been trained to do it. Even when listening to others we listen critically – for points that we agree with or don't agree with. Our fine tuning is centred on the weaknesses in the argument. I wonder how often the baby is thrown out with the bath water because the strength of a proposal is not looked for and therefore not seen?

That paradigm of evaluating is utilized when we make assessment of others. I am not saying that we don't consider strengths, I am saying that our attention is more easily attracted to what ought to be corrected rather than developed. Think about your colleagues, co-workers, families and friends. What is it about them that comes to your attention first?

Recognizing Strengths in Others

If we learn to notice our own hidden strengths, we could then know what to look for and what to develop in ourselves. And in others. The traditional approach assumes that top and full performers have the same characteristics but to different degrees. This is not the case. I have worked with personnel officers who have developed strength in empathizing with everyone in the organization. Other human resource professionals who are struggling to correct their weaknesses in empathic communication refer to compliance, company policy and budgets.

Excellent teachers treat their pupils as equals who will achieve even more than they themselves have. Poor teachers present information to be memorized. People who love their work are not even aware of the clock, poor workers are more focused on what they don't have to do. To the good coach or manager winning means doing things right, improving the individual. To the average coach or manager winning is defined as getting the better score or bottom-line figure.

When we focus on weaknesses, it takes over our evaluation and smothers our perception of strengths. We start to feel sorry or sometimes annoyed or frustrated at someone's weaknesses. We offer pity and often criticism, which can lead to resentment as an individual's weaknesses are seen as an impediment to the team's growth. The development of leadership at every level of an organization will be created more effectively with the philosophy of aligning individuals to focus solely on their areas of strength. The practice of recognizing strengths in others can only follow the principle of recognizing them in ourselves first. If we understand that our attention will be drawn first to the attributes, anxieties and insecurities that we see in ourselves, we must therefore seek to put our own 'observation' in order before we seek to put others where we feel they would be best suited. If not, we are in danger of assuming what is right for them.

If, for example, a manager with a scarcity mentality evaluates a hardworking and ambitious individual, he or she will assume that this person also has a scarcity mentality. Consequently, this person is kept down, however unconsciously, so as not to threaten the security of the manager's own position. If we do not trust ourselves, we cannot trust others, and empowerment will be limited to ensure the status quo is maintained. Because of this restricted paradigm the potential of the individual, the manager and the company is not released.

If the paradigm of interviewing and evaluating everyone on the basis of doing your job could be adopted, the results would be dramatic. In order to receive you have to let go. By holding on tightly you lose. By developing others you yourself develop further. But by holding others down, you atrophy, as a state of neutral does not exist. There is only opening and closing, opposition and alliance, acceptance and rejection.

Opening and closing are natural principles that can be observed in natural phenomena. Knowing when to speak and when to remain silent is part of this. In the East there is tremendous breadth of meaning associated with Yin and Yang, compared with the relative narrowness of popular Western usage. A centuries-old aphorism states: 'Using Yang to act means development of character, using Yin to be still means development of the body.' Using Yang to seek Yin means developing Virtue, using Yin to crystallize Yang means exercise of power. The mutual seeking of Yin and Yang depends on opening and closing. This may be interpreted as 'quiet sitting'. Listening to conscience and observation (ingoing) and alignment to Universal Principles and virtues (outgoing) is necessary for balance and effectiveness. Yin and Yang modes are switched on and off according to what is needed. Shutting down is used to make sure of people's sincerity when it is necessary to see whether their loyalty or interest is based on truth or principle or on enthusiasm fuelled by personality gratification, such as the enjoyment of giving and receiving attention.

People may be drawn to organizations by prospects of success and reward, or they may be drawn by a sense of affinity of aims and ideals, or they may be drawn by admiration or faith. It is essential to understand the nature of the attraction in order to understand the character of those involved. To work effectively with others, particularly in a supervisory or leadership capacity, it is important to understand the mentalities involved so as to be able to predict the pattern of response.

Through inward and outward stillness you become able to listen to others without influencing what they say by your reactions. The speech of others is movement, your own silence is stillness. When statements are inconsistent, if you reflect and enquire introspectively then an appropriate response will be forthcoming. Asian business people and politicians do this as a matter of course; Westerners who do not understand what is happening tend to think they are typical 'inscrutable

Orientals'. To use stillness to listen to what is being voiced means to exercise the ability developed through self-observation to look at matters from all angles by virtue of entertaining no mental fixation or attachments which will affect your perception and understanding.

When a company is being built it only has time to concentrate on its strengths. When it matures, however, it concentrates on making things right – it looks to fixing its weaknesses. Resources must be spent on what people are good at and not wasted on what they are not good at, otherwise a company loses its edge. The most valuable discoveries leaders shaping their company can make are their own strengths and those of others. And strengths can be drawn from childhood yearnings, not just current abilities. It is important whilst scanning for them to look within yourself.

Strengths first start in the mind. Yearnings develop which are characterized by the preferred attraction of one activity over another. The feeling of wanting to do something is triggered when you watch somebody else do it and say to yourself: 'Hey, that's not bad, I wouldn't mind doing that.' Being your own boss can be a common yearning, though this must be coupled with other strengths involving that particular kind of business.

In becoming aware of yearnings, listen to your conscience to ascertain whether they are misleading. Glamour, excitement and power make many yearn for a certain position and can distract them from their real strengths. Where little importance is attached to the mission of a company and its people, it is viewed as a means to an end and we are back to the problem of not aligning goals and values to guiding principles. Your true strengths are an indication of what you are to do. By developing your conscience you discover, build and hone these strengths in line with character-building principles in order to achieve your full potential by doing what you enjoy most.

This natural process is simple when followed, but most of us are not motivated in this way. We can be motivated by the 'friendly' advice of others, or even 'lucrative job offers' which sound appealing and may be financially rewarding but take us away from what we are to do.

If we ignore our true strengths we end up doing what others think is best for us.

When this happens our work is viewed as just work and we plan 'breaks' away from it whenever we can.

There have been many occasions when I have noticed individuals who are 'happy' because it is the end of the week; they have finished work and are now able to 'enjoy' themselves. When 'I have to work' becomes 'I am my work', a release does not have to be sought, it is already there. It is not how hard you work but how you feel about your work and how much of yourself you really put into it.

Where there is an atmosphere of instability and insecurity people can feel alienated from their companies; they question why they should invest themselves wholeheartedly in their work when there is no guarantee that they will be staying. Many reframe their thinking to view work simply as what they do between weekends. With that thinking your work isn't really you – it's just what you do in order to earn. Without commitment there is no achievement. Commitment is not something you manufacture, you discover it. It manifests itself when what you do is what you want. It is increased by doing what you want, by doing what you enjoy – and excelling at it.

Following your strengths aligns your commitment with your purpose by utilizing your potential. How much would you rate your commitment to what you do? In hours, in money or in how much you want to do it? The process of understanding yourself and others is completely interrelated by doing what is right for you, not simply doing the right things. The whole upwardly spiralling process develops your effectiveness, strengths, balance, direction and communications.

As long as we burden ourselves with self-justification and rationa-lies-ing, we are not free to respond to the voice of conscience. One of the most liberating experiences in life is to make the commitment to respond simply to conscience. Those who try it, even for a week, are literally amazed at the release and at how much time and energy have been spent in justifying actions contrary to conscience.

Don't seek your security in being incredibly busy, in your profession, in recognition for talent, in relationships or in anything external. Seek it in your own basic integrity to conscience and principle. Don't allow external factors to become more important to you than doing what you deeply feel you should do. Only when you let go of external sources of security and draw on the security from your own deep inner life, will you be free to do what really matters most.

FOURTH: A Sense of ...

COMMUNICATION

In understanding ourselves, our perceptions and prejudices, we have greater understanding and meaning in our communications with others. The very nature of communicating with ourselves through listening to our inner world has a direct mirroring effect on our interpersonal abilities in our external world. The principle is the same for listening as it is for evaluating and they are interrelated. You cannot evaluate others effectively until you have mastered the art of self-observation in order to understand yourself, and you cannot communicate effectively with others unless you are yourself.

Being yourself is the first and most important step in effective communication.

Through the process of listening to others a large percentage of our hearing is overrun by a constant evaluation of the incoming messages we are receiving. 'Do I agree with this or that? Why are they saying this or that? Why don't they make their point? What is it that happened to me that is similar? That tie doesn't suit them.' And so on. We literally hold two conversations at once.

Constant internal chatter creates a 'fullness' where an

emptiness is required. Where is the usefulness in a vase for flowers? It is in the empty space that receives them and not the pleasant facade. Learn to see the emptiness. When you enter an empty house can you feel the mood of the place which is communicated to you? When a group of people sit in a circle, it is the climate or the spirit in the centre, the empty space, that determines the nature of the group's atmosphere. In the same way that we do not hear our inner higher self whispering to us in the silent gap between our thoughts, due to our internal dialogue, we miss important elements of what is being related to us by others. What is missed is constantly being 'compensated' for by evaluating with our own interpretations.

Four Levels, Eight Gates

In the first chapter I made the point that we often have to hear something, particularly a new idea, several times before it sinks in. The paradigm filter through which we interpret incoming information has been shaped by our conditioned thinking. Interrelated with this, however, is the fact that our sense of hearing is not just one sense. It comprises four senses, each one at a different level. We hear on the physical level, the emotional level, the mental level and the spiritual level. Whereas a mouth is a mechanism by means of which we can open or close feelings or ideas, our ears and eyes are the assistants of the mind and heart, a means of seeing what is really meant. When they act in harmony, all eight senses act as gateways enabling us to really listen to what is being said, rather than merely hearing superficially.

When you first hear something you hear it on the physical level. You hear the actual words, the softness or loudness created by the vibration of speech. Then you hear the feeling, belief and enthusiasm in the words at your emotional level. At the mental level you notice what is important to you and you may make a mental note or write it down – you heard the words intellectually and mentally, your mind worked out what was said and you understood. Much of our schooling ensured that we all hear very well at the mental level. The next level is the spiritual one. How do you know when you hear something spiritually? We often do this without realizing what is happening. It works something like this. Somebody may say something to you which you don't really understand, yet it seems to make sense. Although you have no means of verifying what was said, inwardly you know that it is correct. In fact, what happens is that what you heard reminds you of something. The spoken word suddenly wakes you up to what you already know. These words awaken an area of consciousness that has been dormant for a long time. The fact is that there is nothing new in the world. It has always existed, it is just a matter of waking up and discovering what is already known.

To hear spiritually, at the highest level, is the ultimate step you need to take. When you hear spiritually you enter the final stage of hearing and you know you know. At this level you do occasionally hear something that gives you a feeling that what you hear 'makes sense'. It is a strange feeling because it feels right even though you have never heard it before. You have a flash of illumination as its truth dawns on you. Now open yourself to accepting the premise that if everything is already known through the conduit of the collective unconsciousness, to quote Jung's term, or 'oneness' to state the Eastern term – when we hear something that we 'already know' – the all-knowing deeper spiritual level remembers and recognizes it.

Whenever you are playing a role it is not possible to utilize all eight levels of hearing and seeing, because part of your attention is diverted. It is diverted to ensure that your role is not 'discovered' by the person you are communicating with. You may not even be aware of this as it is an automatic response, but it has a dramatic effect on your ability to listen. Ask yourself: 'Do people communicate by what they say, or do they communicate by how they feel about what they say?' What do you think?

Can you remember a time when you were listening to someone and no matter how fluent or persuasive they were, there was something missing, something you just could not put your finger on? Actions do speak louder than words and our words and actions are two exterior manifestations of our inner thoughts. But most people's words exceed their actions and when they do something it just does not seem right.

Beyond Tuition

Effective communication goes way beyond the variety of 'listening skills' that are learned through tuition. True communication involves intuition where more is communicated by what is not said, the empty parts or silence. Westerners particularly feel uncomfortable when there are periods of silence in the conversation. They therefore usually prepare their reply as the first speaker is winding up. This internal dialogue is amplified when what is being said strongly opposes the listener's own point of view.

Effective communication requires a full understanding and appreciation of the other person's world. To do this you listen with your eyes and heart as well as your ears. Most people tend to think that listening means listening critically. Because they are searching for what they agree or disagree with they feel they are paying attention. They then prepare an answer with their own opinions drawn from their own circumstances.

Clever listening skills may have taught the individual to stay quiet while another person is talking, nodding and 'mmmm-ing' as appropriate to show that he or she is listening, and, of course, not interrupting. This also gives the listener time to adapt a reply in order that it may be accepted by the other person. If something is wanted from the other person the reply tends to put the 'disagrees' to one side and organize the 'agrees' in a pack to give back. If something is not wanted, various opinions on 'What I think you should do' are given, depending on the situation. On both occasions people listen from within their own experience. And this is the root of most communication problems. Because we see the world as we are, not as it is, we do not listen with empathy.

Psychologists use the term 'empathy' to mean understanding how others feel based on how *they* see their world, not on how we see their world. It means moving into the minds and hearts of others to see the world as they see it. To 'know how someone feels' is sympathy, and the paradigm of efficient thinking responds with 'I know how you feel, let me tell you about my experience in order that you can solve your problem'. Often when talking with another we can't wait to get our point over to sort out their problem and to tell them how we sorted out a similar problem.

Our conditioning has taught us to believe that we must get our point in first, particularly during an argument. The way we see it is all that matters. After all, we believe it is the way it is, or the way it happened. We believe that taking the time to listen to another while not defending, attacking or judging, portrays acquiescence and agreement with their viewpoint. The paradigm of getting our viewpoint over has developed the habit of wanting to state how we feel first, and then continuing to restate our opinions until the other person accepts them as theirs. Listening to others to understand their feelings is thought to denote weakness. Consequently, when this is done, the 'dialogue of the deaf' takes over and there is so much internal chatter that there is no listening at all.

In order to have others understand us and listen to us we have to listen to them first.

**When there is high trust and confidence
we can almost communicate without
words. When trust is low, communication
is exhausting and ineffective.**

Without trust and confidence words will not be sufficient to communicate meaning because meanings are not found in words. They are found in people. Trust and confidence need to be communicated first. Here the phrase 'People don't care how much you know until they know how much you care' runs true.

By genuinely wanting to understand how the other person feels first you are showing by your actions that you are seeking to understand. The key to effective communication is trust, and the key to trust is trustworthiness, which is developed by

living your life by the principle of integrity. Your actions expressed in accordance with this principle confirm how you think. As with all natural processes there is no quick fix or short cut and if you genuinely follow the age-old principle of listening before you speak, your actions of trustworthiness will build trust.

Seeking to understand first means diagnosing before prescribing. If you went to a doctor, would he give you a prescription before diagnosing your ailment or problem? Would he say 'I know just how you feel, it happened to me once and this is how I dealt with it'? Would you feel confident if he prescribed for you what was good for him? Are you a clone? Will someone else's autobiography be suitable for you? Yet we behave exactly like this with family, friends and colleagues.

Think of the times you have spoken to your colleagues in this way. Imagine the scenario. A middle manager might notice that his young accounts clerk is bothered about something. 'What's the matter?' he asks. The clerk wants to talk but is loath to say, but after his boss promises genuinely to listen he is persuaded to tell him what the problem is. When the manager hears that the young man is not enjoying his job he exclaims: 'I don't believe it, you don't know how lucky you are to have a job in a firm like this. When I started out it was terrible – antiquated company procedures, manual typewriters, no computers. It's all so much easier now. And remember how many young people don't have jobs at all! If you would just try harder, like young Harrison, you'd see it was a good position and you would like it more. Just stick at it and you won't have a problem.' After a pause he adds, 'Now is there anything else you wanted to talk to me about?'

The manager has prescribed but not fully diagnosed. He knows *best* because he is older and wiser and therefore further discussion is not necessary. Quite simply he has been there and done it and in his mind he is right. It is efficient but is it effective? Will the clerk want to 'discuss' things in the future? The manager has succeeded in making him feel 'ungrateful', although from the clerk's world there is no comparison – his world is as he sees it. In future the clerk will become 'un-communicative' on the subject and his frustration will come out in different ways.

Later, when their relationship lacks open communication, the manager may think 'Why won't he open up, I have always listened to him in the past?' The clerk, on the other hand, will think 'Why open up, he'll only tell me I have never had it so good and go on about what he would do, or compare me with someone else.'

Understanding how people feel about themselves is the real key to using their strengths and releasing their potential.

How individuals feel about themselves is largely a function of how others communicated with them.

Developing Empathy and Trust

Ask yourself: 'How much of the time and energy in my family or business is spent in some kind of defensive or protective communication? How much of my energy with my family and customers is wasted with internal squabbling and interdepartmental backbiting, politics and interpersonal conflicts?' Most people admit that about a third of their time is spent in these destructive ways.

To reduce this destructive element in communication, manipulation, departmental rivalry, contest and positioning, businesses tend to look to new courses on how to improve communications. These initiatives, which focus on listening skills and developing effective work teams, are well intentioned but are resisted by cultures that have fed on themselves for so long that cynicism impedes their potential. Efforts to improve communications have little permanent value unless unifying principles are developed as a foundation on which they can grow.

That foundation lies with people and relationships. When we ignore the foundation, our improvement initiatives are shortlived. Effective communication is built on trust, which is based on trustworthiness rather than positioning, scoring points or politics. Where there is high trust we don't have to watch what we say, the relationship has a strong foundation. When relationships are not strong, people become suspicious and distrustful and watch what they say in case they are misunderstood and give offence.

Effective interpersonal communication requires correct interpretation of meaning and content. Although they are like two languages, both logic and emotion are essential to this. The language of emotion is far more powerful and motivating than its counterpart, logic. That is why it is so important to listen primarily with our eyes and heart and secondarily with our ears. The meaning of communication must be understood first without prejudice, without rejection of content. We can do this by being patient, seeking first to understand and openly express in feelings.

Developing the skills to be effective must follow the same principles associated with developing any other skill. You cannot experience France by reading about France, you have to go there. You cannot learn a skill overnight. You have to progress sequentially through increasing levels of interactive proficiency. The catalyst is the desire to be a good communicator. The strategy is being patient with others as well as yourself.

It is important to take time to understand deeply the content and context in all our interpersonal relationships. Communication is about mutual understanding. We have to learn to say what we mean and to understand what others mean. In this way our ability to see the world, not only through others' eyes but also through their hearts and minds, is developed. When we react through ego to put forth our ideas rather than respond with understanding, we misunderstand and mistrust motives.

When we rush to learn under the paradigm of efficiency, there is no time for deep conversation, for interacting with others in a meaningful way. Under the expediency factor, by wanting it now rather than waiting, we do what is fast and easy rather than what is hard and necessary. Learning is superficial when we are into skills, methods and techniques without understanding the principles that empower us to act in a variety of situations.

Changing into highly effective empathic communicators does not necessitate a series of courses. It requires a new paradigm – a paradigm that diminishes our ego and replaces it with an ability to respond always from our true selves. By attempting to please everyone we are living with the illusion of independence. We communicate efficiently to satisfy the fast-pace 'quick result' paradigm that has created a massive imbalance in our society. This is somewhat removed from the quality of long-term relationships that only effective communication can provide.

It is a fact that our quality of life is, by nature, determined by the quality of our relationships. They provide us with our greatest joy and our greatest sorrow. The 'I' can only be developed through the 'We'. Insincerity is shallow and noticeable, sincerity is deep and reassuring. Being yourself, being sincere with yourself, is the most powerful conduit the 'I' can have for the 'We'. When we become sincere with others, openness and trust builds and communication is developed with or without words. Words have no meaning, people do.

More is communicated in the moment before you speak than in the ten moments that follow.

Remember this next time you talk to someone you have never met before.

Communication is distorted dramatically by our beliefs, as our sense of identity is often inextricably intertwined with them. Any confrontation of a belief is often experienced as a personal attack. Imagine that a person's knowledge and experience on particular subjects are like planets. The nearer the planets are to the sun, with the sun acting as the ego, the hotter they become.

The heat represents the amount the ego identifies with the subject. Two individuals look at differences as though they are

on opposite sides of a huge lens, one side concave, the other convex. For many of us communication is wanting to be understood and if we listen at all it is only with intent to reply. In the above illustration the individual on the left is not very well informed but feels very strongly about what he does know. The other is informed and quite cool about what he knows.

Even if they agree on a belief Mr Hot may be incensed that the other is non-committal about a subject he knows so much about: 'Why doesn't he feel like me?' If they don't agree, Mr Hot will find it difficult to listen at all due to the amount of internal dialogue that he is feeling. His ears and mind will be closed and he will not be able to bring himself to see the other's point of view: 'I don't want to hear it.' He believes he is being attacked personally. It is amazing how we can be so unaware of how we develop our beliefs, yet defend them with such tenacious passion when another appears to be removing them.

Improving our behaviour and attitude with listening skills will not be effective unless we develop paradigm flexibility in order to climb into another person's world, although doing this is sometimes seen as a threat to our own centrally held and emotionally deep beliefs. If we see, appreciate and feel what another person feels, what will happen to our own beliefs and opinions? The humility of principles removes this kind of rationalization.

In having evaluated ourselves through self-observation and attained an understanding of how we think and perceive and how we are controlled by principles, we become more concerned by *what* is right rather than *who* is right in our communications. We value other people and we recognize that their conscience is also a repository of correct principles. Both perspectives have value and when both people understand both perspectives, instead of being on opposite sides of the table, looking across at each other, they find themselves looking at solutions together.

No matter how different another's point of view, each time you catch yourself saying that you cannot understand someone ask yourself if you are stuck in your own world and not appreciating the psychological reality of the other person's world. When it comes to trying to change other people's hotly-held viewpoints, don't argue against their perspective, go and stand where they are standing to see as they do.

The Seven Principles for Good Communications

1 We cannot communicate more than what we are. The precept must be to understand who we are in order to recognize who others are. It follows that being yourself is the key to effective communication. Pleasing everybody by playing appropriate roles is not healthy communication.

2 We need to understand that communication is not simply words, it is the ability to transmit successfully and receive clearly the feelings which are the manifestations of how people think. We communicate as much, if not more, by our silence as by our speech.

3 Communication must be unconditional. Assumptions, prejudices and opinions must be put aside while truly listening.

4 Effective communication must align to the principle of integrity in order to develop the openness and trust that are fundamental to relationships. The lower the trust, the lower the degree of communication (for example, avoiding eye contact).

5 Know where we are coming from by questioning our beliefs in order to understand how they may distort our communications with others. We can then appreciate where others are coming from.

6 Learn that the skill of effective communication follows the sowing before reaping principle: listen before speaking. Where the mouth is the mechanism, the ears and eyes are assistants of the heart and mind. When these three respond in harmony, they act in a beneficial way. To listen primarily with eyes and heart and secondarily with ears, means listening on four levels: physical, emotional, mental and spiritual.

7 Seek to understand. Speak to be understood.

FIFTH: A Sense of ...

MISSION

Any vision or mission that you have for a business will be lost unless you are able to communicate it to others effectively. The two principles that underline the business philosophy that I refer to as 'alternative business thinking' are the two tenets that appear throughout this book.

The first is that you develop from the inside out. You have to put your own house in order before you can advise others to do so, and you have to look to understand your own thinking, evaluations and communications before you look to others. 'Others' in your external world will then be naturally influenced by your example. When you become internally driven by becoming confident in who you are you are no longer externally influenced by certain events. You operate under a 'doing what is important' paradigm, rather than an 'attending to what is urgent' paradigm.

The second tenet is that of 'oneness'. You do not segment your roles or hats into family, company and society at large. The same rules apply to your family, company or organization, regardless of size. The excuse, 'Ah, but this is business', should not apply as how can you suddenly shelve your integrity or values?

The Company Mission

Increasingly, businesses are taking the time to develop missions – a statement which encapsulates what they are about, why they are about, where they are going and how they are going to get there. Sadly it is too often a statement of purpose crafted by senior management in accordance with 'We ought to have a mission statement, in case someone asks'. I wonder how many companies were really seeking a quality creditation in order to give them a competitive edge rather than fully embracing the spirit of a true mission. And I wonder how many companies, after having received the 'talisman' symbol of quality to obtain business, slowly reverted to the old system of doing things.

The bottom line of the mission statement is that if you don't know where you are going, how will you know when you get there? Unless a mission statement is genuine and bought into by the entire organization, what is its value? Macbeth's 'It is a

tale ... full of sound and fury, signifying nothing' is appropriate in this instance. Do you know your company's mission statement? Were you involved in it's formulation? Do you appreciate and understand the 'hard' process that was involved in it? Do you fully buy into it? If not, do you know why? Is it looked upon as a guiding constitution that evokes pride in you? Or does it just hang on a wall in reception evoking disillusionment, fatigue and cynicism. No involvement, no commitment.

The Personal Mission

Has your company got a mission statement? If so, and rather more importantly, have you got your own personal mission statement? Does it align your values with those of your company? Personal mission is rare, so rare that when we experience it, we refer to that person as having a certain something or *je ne sais quoi*. Personal mission is rare because we, as a society, do not promote it. We promote the development of goals to further our careers, but rarely are they strategies which form part and parcel of our own personal mission. Can you imagine the sense of belonging and the security you would enjoy if you had established your own personal mission statement with its own guiding principles?

What exactly is a company? Is it alive or is it a legal document? Does it encapsulate into a unified entity all the ambitions of those who formulated it, or is it a vehicle to just do what you are currently doing? Would you want to work wholeheartedly for a company that did not have a clear idea of its beliefs, values, direction, goals and ambitions? The answer is probably no. You want to be part of something that knows where it is going and is confident in its ability and development to do so.

Let's reverse the situation. Imagine you are a company, totally autonomous and able to make your own decisions.

Would you employ someone who, although ambitious, hardworking and appropriately qualified, had no sense of personal belonging or security and had not created a personal mission statement reflecting his or her beliefs, values and purpose?

You probably wouldn't have confidence in a company that didn't know what it stood for, so should a company have confidence in the individual who doesn't know what he or she stands for?

If you don't know what you stand for, you're in danger of falling for anything. On the principle that we must develop from the inside out, I believe that it is important to develop our personal mission in order that we are able to align it to any corporate mission statement that our company has developed. The process is difficult as it is emotionally and spiritually searching. Those who do so, however, fully understand and appreciate the value that is derived.

Before moving on, take a few moments right now to go through the flow chart opposite.

Have you arrived at a point where you want to develop your own personal mission statement or review your current one?

The Personal Mission Statement Workshop at the end of this chapter will help you to do this. Do take time to answer these questions. Your mission must mean the world to you, but in order to do so, deep reflective time must be invested in its creation. Only you must answer the questions. Too often when facing something of personal importance we confide in others for their considered views. By all means 'bounce' certain

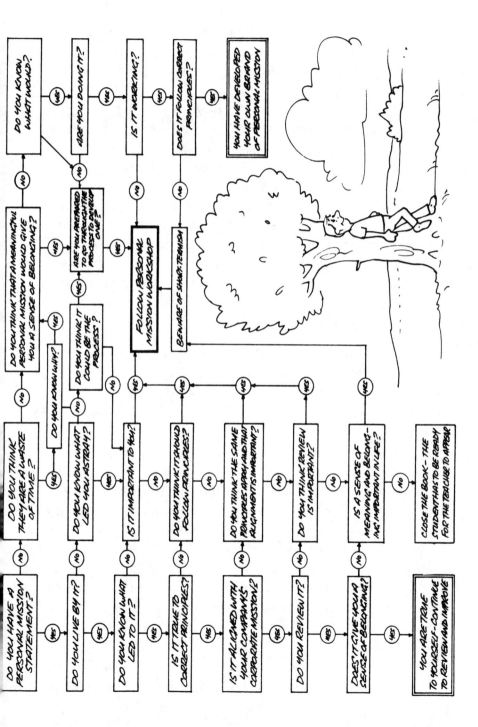

thoughts off others as this will help crystallize your own think-ing about how you feel. Your family, friends and colleagues are agencies, not sources. The only true source for you is your own intuitive self.

Your mission is designed to utilize your greatest strengths, which in turn continue to develop within its framework. Your mission will be the very essence of why you are doing what you do. All the goals you set will be stepping stones towards it. Whereas goals are bounded by time and continue to be replaced by new goals, a mission is timeless and the benefits it creates often extend beyond your life. Many companies have a mission to be number one in their particular field; that, however, is not a mission statement, it is a company goal. A true mission has to express the company's purpose for existence and often becomes the guiding invisible force that unites everyone involved and drives them forward.

**Your mission will be the very essence
of why you are doing what you do.**

For a mission to be personal it has to encapsulate the passion of your own vision, not someone else's. Many attempting to write a mission statement for the first time often write to please or impress another. Often its only usefulness is as a 'to do' list which has been drawn up and can now be filed away. In a business sense this is what happens when a mission statement comes down from the boardroom on 'Mount Olympus'. After being attended to by the word processor in the PR department it ends up hanging on a wall instead of living in the hearts and minds and lives of all those who are involved, directly or indirectly.

Why should people embrace something they have not been involved with? To go back to your personal mission, which is what your life is about, there are two significant factors. You must have a vision of yourself and your future and you must clarify your values. The whole process of developing a mission statement cultivates the passion you feel for your vision and empowers you to work towards it.

Imagination

The tool to develop your vision is imagination. Everything that has ever been created began as an idea. We create what we imagine. Too often we jam our creative imaginations with self-limiting beliefs and negativity. We concentrate on what is urgent. Other people's priorities and any visions we have tend to be based on our illusory perceptions reflected from the social mirror. Following social norms instead of principles fails to provide the quality of life we hope for and our choices are based on the expectations of others. We consequently become dis-illusioned with our dreams and our creative imagination withers as our cynicism grows.

That is why being yourself is crucial to developing your vision. The process of imaginative vision is related more to receptivity than to concentrated effort. Struggling and strain-ing to know what to do impedes the process. Like radio waves, ideas are all around us, they fill the air. The ones that coincide with our own desires can be developed by our own strengths and are awaiting our reception. We simply have to open our-selves to receive them. To enhance our receptivity we need to 'go into the silence' or 'stillness' and we do this by spending time alone. (Further details of this process can be found in *Born to Succeed*.) Meditation eliminates the mental noise that blocks inspiration. When open, our minds have the innate ability to receive ideas. Too often we are so sure of how things are that we lose all perspective on how things could be.

Many of us are living out of scripts handed to us by others, scripts which have no contribution from our true selves. Some may be constructive, with 'You're a natural negotiator', others may be destructive, with 'Why can't you be more like your sister'. Either way they serve as an impediment to connecting with who we are and what we are about. We are continually bombarded with the messages and images projected by the media. The main message we receive is that the only important news is bad news.

Over lunch one day, the British broadcaster Martyn Lewis, 'the good news advocate', related how he was briefed to announce on the news that two people had drowned on the *Altamira* passenger ship in the Indian ocean. No mention was to be made of the thousand or more people whose lives had been saved due to the incredible bravery of the rescue services in bad weather. Martyn made the point that this reflected the mindset of the journalists who were not even aware of what they were discerning. They only saw what they expected to see. Cynicism, scepticism, violence, indulgence, fatalism, and materialism are all images which provide sources for our personal vision. Is it any wonder that many of us feel disconnected and at odds with ourselves?

Where do creative visions come from? When it comes to new ideas there is nothing new under the sun. All ideas already exist, only needing creative imagination to bring them to light. Apples dropping in Newton's garden were the catalyst that brought him to an understanding of the principle of gravity. Seventeen years later he encapsulated this knowledge into a law and brought it to light. The principle had always existed, but people had to be made aware of it in order to utilize its benefits.

Fire existed before its capacity was realized. Under certain conditions, electricity and gas create power, but the sources of this power have always been available. Leonardo da Vinci imagined the submarine and helicopter 400 years before other ideas brought them into existence. The property and action of the law of displacement was operative long before Archimedes took his famous bath. Ignorance of an existence does not mean non-existence.

Every individual who has brought to the attention of others the existence of an idea and the benefits that can be obtained from an awareness of it, has been awarded, grudgingly or appreciatively, the accolade: 'He's his own man' or 'They're true to themselves' or 'She's certainly an individual'. Those who are themselves become receptive to the universal ideas that are available in abundance. Mostly they are as surprised at their discovery as everyone else. The 'Eureka!' they exclaim is from the dawning realization that what they have is what they are searching for. Being yourself and having a personal mission to re-affirm what you want keeps you on track and relaxes the stranglehold of the conscious over the subconscious. This allows you to tap into a far deeper and richer well of inspiration.

The illustration on page 98 shows the possible relationship between the timeless realm that contains all ideas and the accepted ideas. The accepted ideas are what have been socially adopted and again have a relationship with all known ideas. Every 'new' idea must experience ridicule and discussion before its adoption, and this process of stages and delay applies to social and spiritual ideas as well as physical inventions. Anything that does not fit or agree with society's currently adopted conventional thinking is perceived as a 'cultural revolution' that will upset the status quo, as discussed in Chapter 1.

Now imagine that each one of us has been born with a specific vocation or mission that only we can do. Imagine that everything in nature is one and the same, that everything is interrelated and adheres to the same fundamental laws and principles; that the laws that affect nature are the same principles that affect us; that the paradigm is one of man with nature, not man against nature. It follows that the strength you were born with will relate to empowering that mission or calling.

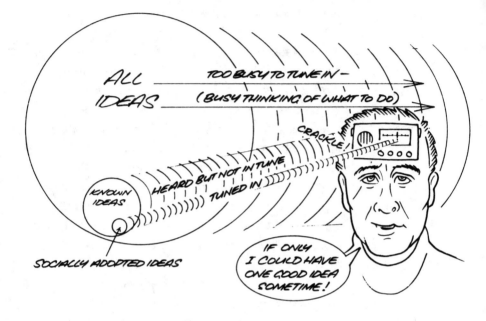

**To the degree that you are yourself, you
are open to receive that which you are to do.**

Similarly, to the degree that you are not yourself, you are closed
to what you are to do.

Metaphysically speaking, you attract the particular wave-
lengths that co-ordinate with your own thoughts. It is vitally
important therefore to be in tune with those vibrations and to
match your own *true* vocation or calling, not your *conditioned*
one. Oscillations that vibrate in harmony are a stronger force.
The laser beam that cuts through steel has the same energy
output as the electric bulb but is highly concentrated. This
principle applies universally.

If you push against the fundamental laws of life, if you

mechanically do something because 'that's what you do', if you do not evaluate and observe the true you and if you do not encapsulate what you want in a mission with clarification of values and what you stand for, then the power of any goals you make will be analogous to that of the electric bulb. The alternative, which makes sense, whether fully accepted at this stage or not, will provide you with power analogous to that of the laser beam.

Finding Your Creative Vision

In attaining strength nature follows a sequential process. It does not jump from seed to sapling, or from spring to sea. It follows a natural growing process which nurtures and continually strengthens. The tiny frail seed becomes a strong living 'adult' in its journey to become a tree. The tiny spring always gets to where it's going. Its issues become part of the huge force of the ocean. Regardless of obstacles it continues to raise itself to the appropriate level to overcome and continue its mission. It cannot move on to a higher level until the lower levels have been attained.

There cannot be a short cut in the continual process of character, family, company or organization development. Each one follows a sequential step. The mission needs nurturing at every step. We cannot nurture something unless we love it. Love is a power greater than ourselves that works through us. We are able to use its pure force to develop what is truly important to us. There is a relationship between love, understanding, appreciation and accomplishment. The way in which you live your life is of great importance to you, your loved ones and, in some significant way, to the world as a whole.

How do you go about discovering the creative vision that already exists within you? When an inspiration hits you, pay attention to it. As you go through the Personal Mission State-ment Workshop pay attention to the ideas that come to you. This is how you develop confidence in your imagination. One step at a time. By acting on your inspirations. Often we ignore our inspirations and then wonder why our lives lack the magi-cal quality we felt when we were children. Inspiration gives birth to further ideas as well as to the actions that make them materialize. It is the ongoing search for ideas that supports and strengthens the original, sometimes ridiculous, idea. Children trust their imagination and are not afraid of being ridiculous. The best ideas are often ridiculous at first.

Whatever anyone thinks of you is none of your business.

You have probably already had many inspirations which you have simply dismissed. That is why it is so important to carry a journal in order to capture your thoughts. When they are gone they seldom return, so you must secure them. A 'Eureka!' is like a slippery fish; you can suddenly wonder what the idea was that you had. I am sure you have experienced that frustration. As you secure the idea by writing it down, a host of others can start to build from the first, one after another. Consideration of these creative ideas actually reconnects you with a vocational and potent source of energy that you may not have utilized to date. In this way you can learn to give expression to the deeper inner reality we all experience.

At the start of your journal write down the following affirma-tion: *I am open to receiving the vision of my life's work, and the more I focus on its manifestation the clearer and more effective my strengths and talents become.* This or a similar type of affirmation will draw your attention towards your inspirations.

Values

Next it is important to know what you stand for and what values are central to your life. Values are universal, cultural and individual. Universal values transcend time, place, language and cultural barriers. They comprise timeless constants about the human condition and are mentioned in all the great works of wisdom: the Bible, the Upanishads, the Bhagavad-gita, the Koran, the Talmud and the Dhammapada. These values remain as relevant today as they always have been. The fact that we still seek to resolve moral dilemmas, wonder at the pyramids, feel awe at cathedrals and works of art, are moved by certain music and identify with Shakespeare's characters, speaks volumes on the mystery of universal values. They can move us out of our various roles and identities into the vast expanse of timeless reality. Today such values as unity, sacrifice, peace, service, God, love and brotherhood receive little attention as we are otherwise occupied with material and economic pursuits.

Cultural values serve to establish and maintain social order. They are reflected in government and law, philosophy and education, language, status systems and social conventions. If all you know is your own culture then you have only met one person. A culture is a manifestation of what people think and feel – the social norms, what is acceptable and unacceptable. When we mistake cultural values for universal values and proclaim them as the 'accepted' doctrine we are aligning ourselves to functional as opposed to arbitrary values.

Just because a cultural value serves a function does not mean it is the only or best way of doing something. But this does happen. We think our way is the right way and align our beliefs with it. When cultures meet there is always conflict as each culture believes that its way is the right way to live. Yet an enlightening cross-pollination often results from their creative interaction. Indeed the meeting of Eastern and Western cultures is currently creating exciting, interesting and unified times. The study of other cultures helps us to see ourselves more clearly and enables us to identify ourselves as part of human-kind, bringing us closer to a realization of 'oneness'. In under-standing other cultures we see clearer universal values which are uniform to the entire human race.

Our individual values are reflected in our personal goals. In fact our goals underline our values system, which is why it is important to know what they are. They are reflected in our relationships with others, the commitments and promises we make, and the kind of preferences we hold. They are the result of our conditioning and experiences. Our values are our own private meanings that we attach to objects, events and ideas, or relationships, and any differences in meaning are down to us.

Two people can respond to the same event in different ways. One who values prestige and recognition may drop a family outing when the opportunity to go to an event attended by 'everybody who is anybody' unexpectedly arises. Another may choose the family event regardless of how influential the sud-den alternative. For this person, established values take the tension out of making those decisions which can cause the 'will I, won't I' dilemma. For this person the action that aligns to values is the only one considered. Attention is given to discuss-ing with the family how their event can be re-arranged, and it may be that the whole family ends up going to the other unexpected event.

Unless we consciously take the time to establish what is important in our lives we robotically operate under a programme created by past experiences. Well-meaning admo-nitions in early personal relationships are projected into our daily life and take on the weight of the individual meaning that we attach to them. For example, a client's rejection of our business may be taken personally because we unconsciously remember a negative and critical parent we tried to please.

Take the time to consider the five most important values in your life. Then write down your reasons.

Value No 1 . . . .

Why? . . . .

Value No 2 . . . .

Why? . . . .

Value No 3 . . . .

Why? . . . .

Value No 4 . . . .

Why? . . . .

Value No 5 . . . .

Why? . . . .

Personal Mission Statement Workshop

An ideal way to focus your thinking on what you are to do in life and to utilize all your creative imagination is to write your own obituary. I first encountered this idea in Charles Handy's *The Age of Unreason* but there are numerous variations on this theme. Imagine that you have just passed on. You have devoted yourself to your life's work and have been successful in all that you planned. What is the legacy that you have left behind you? What were your achievements and what did you contribute for the benefit of others? What will you be remembered for above all? Write in no more than 200 words a statement of what your life was about and what difference it made.

OBITUARY PLAN

What would you want written as a one-sentence epitaph on your tombstone?

EPITAPH

Insight Keys to Creating Your Mission

What did you most want to do in the world when you were a child?

What situation in your world gave you greatest pain as a child?

What is the most exciting thing you have done in your life?

What do you consider your best achievement during your life?

What has been the happiest moment in your life?

What insights do the answers to these questions give you?

Why did you feel the way you did?

Has there been a time when you did something that everyone said you could not do?

What was it?

How did you feel when you had done it?

At what time in your life have you felt most committed?

What made you persist in spite of all obstacles?

What strengths have others noticed in you?

What do you feel are your foremost strengths?

What is your strongest preference which you really enjoy doing?

If you had unlimited time and resources would you do that?

Who are the three people who have made the greatest positive impact in your life?

What qualities of character did they have that you most admired?

Were their characters the reason they had such a significant impact?

Why were they able to have a developing influence on you?

Which activities in your personal life do you hold in the highest esteem?

What hidden talents do you have that others are not aware of?

Is there anything that you would be willing to put everything on the line for?

What would that be and why?

What can you do best that is valued highly by others?

What parts would you like to play in your three favourite films?

Why would you want to be identified with those characters?

Are you satisfied with your current level of activity in the physical area?

What principles would develop the fulfilling results you desire in this area?

Are you satisfied with the current level of activity in your mental needs and capacities?

What principles would develop the fulfilling results you desire in this area?

Are you satisfied with your current level of activity in your social needs and capacities?

What principles would develop the fulfilling results you desire in this area?

Are you satisfied with your current level of activity in your spiritual needs and capacities?

What principles would develop the fulfilling results you desire in this area?

What results are you currently getting in your life which please you?

What paradigms are producing those results?

What results are you currently getting in your life which don't please you?

What paradigms are producing those results?

If you could share one bit of wisdom with the whole world what would it be?

What is your basic philosophy in life?

What are the underlying principles of this philosophy?

What would you really like to be and do in your life?

What are the important principles upon which you are being and doing?

Review all your answers and then write out your life's mission in the space below.

PERSONAL MISSION STATEMENT

. . . .
. . . .
. . . .
. . . .
. . . .
. . . .
. . . .
. . . .
. . . .
. . . .
. . . .
. . . .
. . . .

Now review your statement and condense your personal mission into no more than two sentences.

MY PERSONAL MISSION

. . . .

. . . .

. . . .

Aim to develop a meaningful personal statement that will focus your strengths and talents. Clarify your values and what you want to be and do. Remember that this exercise may involve many hours or even months. Ideally you should go off to a personal retreat for a day or so in order to give it your deep attention. This quest for meaning in your life is too important to be merely 'fitted in'.

Your mission statement should be simple enough to be remembered and frequently reflected upon. It can be as long as you like so long as you can summarize its essence.

Your mission statement does not have to show how it will be accomplished. It is designed to direct and express your values and beliefs. It does not show actual plans; it provides guides not goals.

Writing and developing your personal mission is neither instant nor easy. It is developed contemporaneously with the whole process of questioning your paradigms, self-observation and improvement. Discovering your inner drives and matching them with your activities requires time and commitment. Mission statements can grow out of a strong sense of responsibility stemming from adversity. For example, the disappearance of the British estate agent Susan Lamplugh was the catalyst for her mother's mission to develop the Lamplugh Trust which is dedicated to increasing awareness and protection for women in business. Mission statements that are reviewed regularly become more effective in the same way that regular exercise becomes more enjoyable. To have a mission statement only on paper is worse than having no mission at all. The only result will be guilt. Put a mark in your diary or calendar so you can review it on a monthly basis. Isn't it worth spending 30 minutes a month with your personal guide?

The foundational principles which characterize the most powerful mission statements are transcultural. They share universal values and represent the deepest and best within you. They embody both ends and means, vision and values respectively, developed from conscience guidance towards principles. They integrate the needs and capacities of the physical, social, mental and spiritual dimensions. And they are written to inspire you, the creator, not to impress others. Your mission statement communicates what is important to you and inspires you to set about it. Mission gives purpose to life. It adds meaning to what you do and in its purest form it is so deeply felt that it explains why you do what you do.

Lacking a mission, people tend to have only materialistic goals. And when goals are achieved the refrain is often: 'Is that all there is?'

Goals and action plans develop best in the framework of a guiding mission.

It is highly important that these factors follow the rules. (If you wish to know more about the process of goal setting and action planning refer to *Born to Succeed*.)

It is also vitally important to establish the right order: your

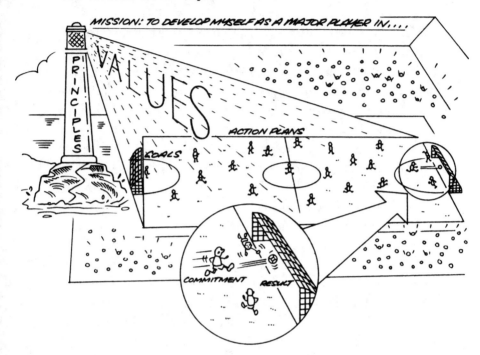

mission with its guiding principles, your values, your goals and your action plans and strategies, your rewards and your commitment.

The Value of Mission

Your mission statement is a general statement about why you are here on earth. As the achievement of your goals begins to realize your mission, your horizons will expand as your capacities continue to expand. The test to find out whether your mission on earth is finished is simple: if you are alive it isn't. It will grow with you. Our mindset often looks for finite ends to everything but that is what we have goals for. If your mission becomes a glorious goal then what do you do when you have achieved it? OK, you stop and enjoy it. Then what? How long do you stop for? Getting elected or becoming prime minister or getting where you want to go is only one goal in the achievement of a mission.

The missions to put men in space and on the moon were goals. Does the real mission stop there? I labour this point because many people have approached me with a disillusionment based on the belief that if it is never attainable why bother in the first place? The mindset dictates that it must be measurable. Why, and by what standard? How can you measure intangibility, character strength or spiritual enlightenment? If you put a measure on your mission you are limiting yourself and your beliefs. Use your goals to measure your progress. Use your mission as a guide to empower you and give you a reason for being. Do you want your reason for being quantified? Do you want to know that you made a difference in ten, one hundred or one thousand lives? How can you quantify the difference you make even in one person's life? That value is measureless.

Now that you have drawn up your own mission statement, you can develop or review one for your family, company or organization. You will now be able to view these with new understanding and appreciation. Is there some input that you can make? Do your values, beliefs and philosophy align with your company's? You may think that this subject is not even approachable, that the company has developed one already and will not look favourably on some 'know-all' making suggestions. But you would be surprised how much difference one person who genuinely cares about a company can make.

I remember one executive from a major organization resenting a review of the mission statement. He said, 'Look, Colin, we have spent a great deal of time developing what we have got and we don't want to change it now. It's done.' I replied that I was very happy with that if he truly was too. When asked what I meant I suggested that he tell me his commitment to his mission statement on a scale of one to ten. After a lengthy pause he replied seven. We talked and he understood that what he had developed was the basis for what his company was in existence for. The development of a mission statement must not be perceived as a cost but an investment. And moreover, any future review or enhancement of it should be done with the genuine volition and participation of all those affected by that statement. Its monitoring should not be viewed as a time and a cost task to be done but, rather, as a participating nurturing exercise to be enjoyed. If a company loses its *raison d'être* where is it going?

The importance of the company mission statement is one that encapsulates and reflects the needs of all those it touches. For the customers, clients, people, products, owners and investors, it is the essential key to long-term organization and fulfilment and continued development and growth. Its regular enhancement is in direct proportion to the improved effectiveness of those involved. The paradox of increased focus within broadening horizons is experienced.

As well as being meaningful, inspiring and motivating, the statement must have both means and ends, values and vision, and can also include the guiding principles that the organization adheres to. It must deal with the economic, social, psychological and spiritual needs of those who are involved and thereby committed to it. It must be developed from the very depths of the business in order that it forms the very constitution of that business. In this way everyone who is a part of the organization will be as committed to it – and to the ensuing identified imperatives and strategies – as those who were involved in its original formulation.

A Balanced Solar System

The 'solar system' illustrates how the underlying principle of trustworthiness is first developed at the personal level. Your personal and professional development and goals overlap, thus

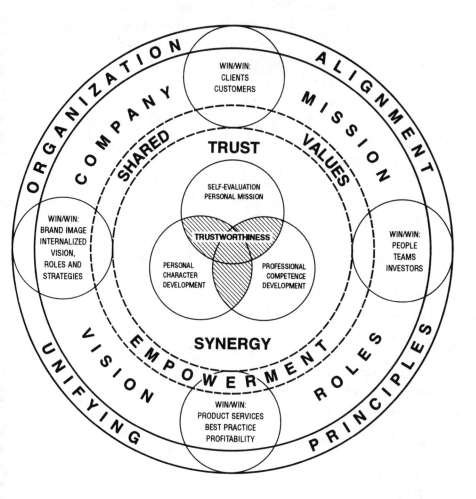

growing out of the principles of integrity, industry and being true to yourself. The outgrowth of this is an atmosphere of trust and synergy conducive to openness and communication. With shared values empowerment can be nurtured. Within the guidelines and parameters of mission, vision, roles and corner-post strategies, empowered individuals and teams can continuously improve their methods. This in turn develops organization alignment that is constantly guided by unifying principles.

We cannot really empower others as empowerment is developed from the inside out. People empower themselves through the development of character, competence and leadership attributes. There is no such thing as organizational behaviour; there is only behaviour of individuals within the organization. Culture is the result of how people think and feel, so an empowering culture must be developed from the inside out. At the very heart of empowerment is trustworthiness; thus an organization becomes trustworthy to the degree that individuals within the organization become trustworthy. The development of what we are and what we do results in character and competence respectively, and both are essential to create trustworthiness.

Trust is the natural outgrowth of trustworthiness and acts as a cohesive to bring everything together. In an environment of trust people look to co-operate to develop 'win/win paradigms' rather than compete on a 'win/lose paradigm'. When empowerment is introduced without the nurturing of individuals' characters and competence – which are what actually drive the organization – the competitive paradigm remains unchanged. People then revert to their old mindset when the pressure is increased.

Empowerment, trust and control are interrelated. To the degree that there is trust, people are empowered and control is diminished. You may think that without trust there needs to be control or chaos will ensue. But control impedes people's potential, so it is important to treat and develop empowerment permanently so that individuals can develop trustworthiness.

When you have trust you have open communication lines and genuine communication systems and strategies can be developed based on win/win agreements. Where integrity, competency and involvement are instrumental in creating shared vision and strategies, we empower ourselves and others. But in these circumstances, who controls and supervises? The win/win agreements developed by self-directing individuals and teams do. If on the other hand people need constant supervision and control then the principle of developing trustworthiness has not been followed. Control may keep the 'traditional' practice of doing something on course – but is it the *best* way?

When every step is checked to ensure that the 'right' way is adhered to, there is no opportunity to improve ways. In a high-trust culture honest mistakes are viewed as an opportunity to learn and grow, which is what they are. If at first you don't succeed, find out why, don't look for who to blame. Communicate and look to what can be learned and move forward. When people are afraid to take risks they are not empowered. If a system is wrong should we look to blame the system or seek to improve the system producers? Incorporating new systems without changing the paradigm will not create the desired long-term results. This is analogous to improving the attitude or behaviour while keeping the same out of date 'map'.

The process of building character and competency involves feedback. And with a clear sense of vision and purpose feedback assists in achieving a greater integrity. It is difficult to ask for feedback and it is even harder to receive it. But our thinking must be aligned to understand that we are not governed by feedback, we are governed by the principles and purposes we have built into our mission statement. Feedback is a powerful tool for developing open communication. The responses of others reflect not only how they see us, but also how well we do those things they feel are all-important to them.

Feedback tells as much about the people giving it as about those who receive it. It is not judgement of another's character, it is feedback against performance and effectiveness criteria. On analysing feedback and comparing the results desired with our performance, we are able to go inside and work on our character – if that's what it takes to receive those results.

Improving Your Best

Obviously there are many challenges in creating empowerment from the inside out. The greatest barrier will be the fixed paradigm of 'this empowerment fad won't last', 'people are more secure when controlled' or 'whoever heard of win/win?' No quick fix will be sustainable and the process may take months – after all we are developing a proactive rather than reactive culture. Time constraints will be a major factor in only paying lip-service to fundamentals that are indeed the catalyst for positive change.

Although only touched on, the ideas for developing the enormous potential that often lies dormant in a company cannot simply be put to one side as an unobtainable Utopia because the conscience confirms that its fundamental principles are right. The purpose of this book is to provoke thinking sufficiently to take action in the appropriate order – from the inside out. Its purpose is not to back up and persuade. Trying new systems and programmes without shared values and vision encapsulated in a meaningful mission is analogous to bandaging a wound without first setting the bone.

Co-operation and competition are the Yin and the Yang of the global marketplace and your organization's culture is the one competitive advantage that cannot be duplicated. Technology can be copied, investment brought in, information found, but a high-trust, empowered culture is always home grown. And a quality culture can only be nourished by following guiding principles over time. This is true for any group of people, be it a family, company or organization.

I believe all those involved in an organization should develop their own personal mission statements in order that they can clearly see if they genuinely want to work with the company. Without one they will not be aware of how their 'beliefs' guide them and they will merely 'work for' a company. Do they ever feel a part of it? Having a mission statement helps you to achieve success because it answers deep questions like 'what do I want to be and do?' When you identify your essential purpose and set up shared vision and values you can be successful with any situation that comes along.

A mission excites people, permeates an organization and shapes actions. A corporate mission statement bought into by everyone provides meaning.

People want meaning in their lives. It is the essential ingredient in organizational success.

Communication is more effective when there is a shared mission. We cannot communicate more than what we are, and we can never build a company greater than its purpose. By creating and continually reviewing what we are about we ensure that we stay on track and perform to our best each day – a best that continually improves.

A Sample Mission Statement

I have provided my own statement (page 122) to assist you in developing yours.

MISSION STATEMENT

'Inspiring Others To Fulfil Their Potential'

'To inspire people and organizations to realize and fulfil
their potential and significantly increase their effectiveness
in order to achieve worthwhile purposes in their lives.
In this way and by living in accordance with guiding
Universal Principles and Values, I will continue
to develop my own potential.'

Guiding Principles

1 Being true to myself
2 Conducting my business and personal life with uncompromising integrity
3 Influencing and communicating ethics by example
4 Building long-term relationships founded on trust and respect
5 Striving continually to improve my character and competence
6 Seeking to understand others' beliefs and values before being understood
7 Achieving success through developing others

Values

- *Justice and Fairness:* that everyone has the right to be treated equally in humanistic terms
- *Industry and Discipline:* that you cannot respect or evaluate others before you have your own house in order
- *Integrity and Sincerity:* that you keep the promises you make to yourself and others and use no deceit with others
- *Temperance and Moderation:* that you do not overindulge to your detriment and do not overreact in resenting unkindness
- *Frugality and Order:* that you spend less than you earn, waste nothing and let all your activities have their place
- *Silence and Tranquillity:* that you keep your own counsel, avoid trifling conversation and are not disturbed at common or unavoidable accidents

SIXTH: A Sense of ...

CREATIVITY

Your work, what you do, serves as your expression of creativity. That is why time must be taken to develop your mission – a mission which encapsulates your quest for meaning in your life. It doesn't matter what you do so long as it is satisfying to your being and fulfils you. When what you do is not important to you and has no meaning, you shut yourself off from the flow of creativity.

There is an infinite source of creativity available to us and we must learn to become open to it. The process of creating your personal mission brought into use your creative imagination. The stream of thoughts, ideas, experience and wisdom which springs to you is fed by an even greater source, an infinite reservoir of all-knowing wisdom. Knowing how to draw from this reservoir is the key to creativity.

There is only one Universal Law of creation. That law follows the principle that when two opposites or polarities are brought together a third element is created. The obvious and most creative third element is a child, conceived through the communication of two complementary energies – male and female. The male 'active' force interacts with the female 'passive' force, but here understand what is meant by the term force, for in fact a force cannot be passive. Unless two forces come together nothing can be created.

In the East these two complementary energies of active and

passive, outgoing and receptive, are referred to as Yang and Yin. Their meanings go infinitely further than the simple meaning of the male and female physical manifestations that are commonly attached to them. Everything that is created is a result of the interaction of these opposite yet complementary energies. Both are contained within each of us but will only create for us effectively when they are harnessed and balanced.

The Law Of Three

When two individuals discuss ideas together, a third intangible force is created which would not have happened without the first two coming together. This intangible force is the resultant idea.

All the world's religions attach importance to the three elements of creativity. All refer to father, mother and child, although the somewhat masculine-oriented Christian church refers to father, son and holy spirit. Another way of saying father, mother and son, is love, life and light. The father is the masculine love, the mother is the female wisdom or life-force, and when combined they create a child like a great light.

This ancient knowledge helps us to understand the law of creativity. The three syllables of the word 'Israel' come from the following sources: 'Is' from Isis, mother god of 'Egypt' (life), 'El', the male force in almighty Allah Eliom, and 'Ra' the god of light in Egypt (and the result of the interaction of 'Is' and 'el'). You can say that the father moves through the mother to make a child or that the love moves through the life substance to create a light. This triad of the law of creation has permeated through all religions as a basic law of life.

The three distinct parts of love, life and light exist within each of us. The male outgoing love is expressed in what you do in your life, your vocation, what you make available to and share with the world. The female incoming intuitive wisdom is the substance with which you form and shape what you have decided to do. This is your vocation in action. A child is the result of these two energies, creating the 'light' from which the world benefits. In other words, each one of us is a natural-born creator.

By taking your desire for action and channelling it through your intuitive wisdom you create a product, service or benefit. This is your light by which others see you. Light is the metaphor often used to convey the nature of consciousness. As we become conscious of an object it is indeed as if the object has emerged from darkness. 'Let there be light' is not only the central image of creation, it also best epitomizes the nature of our own awareness and level of consciousness.

Through our subjective perceptions we create our own world – the world according to us. Through self-observation and clarification of what is important to us we actually develop a great awareness and en-light-enment of what our life is about in relation to the rest of the world. Enlightenment is the self-realization that a oneness connects everything in the universe. To the degree that we come into this realization do we make it possible for higher sources of creativity to manifest through us.

At the heart of our creativity is intuition, incoming wisdom which flows from the boundless reservoir of infinite intelligence. The ability to go beyond the islands of given information into the sea of pre-conscious thought and return with knowledge that somehow enables new connections or new insights – to be established and perhaps communicated to others – is the essence of human potential. Regardless of our endeavours in any field, intuition is our most valuable guide. Reason may sharpen our understanding of ideas but intuition alone reaches to new knowledge.

By living the life we consciously choose for ourselves our

work becomes our vocation. By following our conscience and being true to ourselves, we naturally align ourselves to principles. By accepting that these principles guide us we become more and more receptive to the incoming intuitive wisdom that is available to us and that had before simply passed through us. In this way we become aware of how to put our deep desires into right action, and the light of our fruits clears the way for us to see them even further.

To work in harmony with all the higher laws and forces is to put in motion a sequence of events that always works in conjunction with us. This is the secret of success. All our best ideas come when we least expect them – when we're driving, walking, playing, relaxing, or in the bath. When our mind is no longer having to work with the constraints that we have imposed upon our thinking, it is free to act fully in our interests and introduce new perspectives. This is our natural thinking working for us. We don't have to force it and certainly it should not be a rare occurrence.

Four Levels

Thoughts are subtle, vital and creative forces which continually shape our lives according to their nature. Our thoughts build the world that we live in and most of the time we cast our mind adrift by worrying about what we should be doing or feeling guilty about what we should have done. Why do we do this?

Each of us has four body levels. First and lowest of all is the physical body, flesh, bones and blood, etc. Second, at a slightly higher level, are feeling and desire. Third, and higher still, is the powerful energy of thinking, the mental body level that affects both our emotions and our physical body. Fourth, the highest and most inner of all, is the spiritual body level, which is perfect. This is the home of intuition, which never makes mistakes. If you activate this level you will automatically cause your mind to think positively, your emotions to be good and your physical body to act correctly.

Think of your body as a car with four cylinders. A four-cylinder car is not functioning properly when one or two of the cylinders are out of action. If this is the case the engine will generate very little power. It is the same with us if our fourth cylinder or our inner spiritual wealth is not functioning. We will create very little power and not function effectively.

Many people, however, function on the lower two cylinders. Their energy in life is concentrated on the two lower levels, the physical and the emotional. They are concerned with physical needs such as having enough food, drink and sleep, and with having enough material possessions and wealth. They are also preoccupied with emotional needs. They desire gratification and want to have power and control over others. Their whole life is concerned with satisfying their central need to satisfy their physical and emotional desires. They hardly ever use their creative minds, and as far as their fourth higher spiritual level is concerned, not only are they unaware of it but in some cases may even deny its existence. It is an unfortunate fact of life that few of us choose to operate our engine to its full potential. Most of us are functioning on only two cylinders – at half power.

The advertising industry understands this reality. All adverts are geared to the physical and emotional levels. Those that are persuading us to buy products appeal to our emotional element. You never see adverts geared to the mental or spiritual level. Only about 10 per cent of people actually use their mental level to think creatively. The other 90 per cent tend to buy the products that this 10 per cent produce, which is why only a small percentage of the world's population are financially wealthy.

If you collected all the money in the world and distributed it equally among all the people in the world it would not be long before the few creative people became very rich once more and the majority returned to abject poverty. The answer for this lies in the way people think.

We may all be born equal with the same faculties, but very few of us exercise them to good purpose.

It is one thing to realize that we have a mind with which to think, but another to know how to use the faculties with which we are born.

As each level has control over the levels below, by utilizing the faculties of our spiritual level, the source of our intuition, we can dramatically increase our life's effectiveness. The key to success is to get all four levels to work in harmony. To do this they must operate in the correct sequence – from the inside out. For example, starting with the inner or spiritual level, where intuitive ideas come from, think of an idea. Then move to the level of the mind, where you can make a picture of your idea. Then add feeling at the emotional level and get excited about it. Finally, action comes from the physical level. This is how the four bodies work together. You start with an idea, you make a picture of it, you add feeling and you take action. A very interesting change takes place when you start to use all four body levels in harmony. Instead of wanting to control others all the time, you begin to appreciate other people. Whereas before you had a selfish desire to exploit others, on a 'what's in it for me?' basis, now you begin to seek ways to serve others. You will start to be less concerned with competition and instead your direction will be focused on co-operation. This sense of co-operation will seek to develop win/win situations rather than win/lose situations. You will genuinely want the person you do business with to profit as much as yourself.

You will also begin to feel less concerned with acquiring things and more interested in giving of yourself. Owning a lot of goods will seem less important and you will become more willing to share with others. You become less focused on your personal self and more concerned with the universal self, and as you become less self-centred you become more principle-centred and develop a feeling of group or collective consciousness. When you are more in tune with others you begin to accept that there are other beliefs. You finally enter into the realization that we are not separate but are all one. This great truth of oneness is the ultimate experience.

Oneness

This conscious realization of our oneness with an Infinite Intelligence removes the limitations that we have set on our own creativity. Everything in the universe operates under immutable laws. But the prime force behind those laws is a Universal Spirit of Infinite Life, Power and Intelligence. Throughout the world numerous names exist for this, but they all refer to the spiritual force known as God. Each of us is an individualized spirit which does not differ in essence or quality from the Infinite Spirit that we are all part of, although there are differences in degree. If God is the Infinite Source from which we come then it follows that to the degree that we are our true selves we have characteristics identical in quality to that source. Just as a drop of water taken from the ocean has the same characteristics as its source.

Does it not then follow that the degree to which we open ourselves to this divine flow determines our creative powers? And if these powers are potentially without limit does it not follow that the only limitation we have is the one we set ourselves by virtue of not knowing or being true to ourselves?

The most powerful medium in our lives is the power of creative thought. Our thoughts always create. They are literally the cause of all the conditions that we experience. Under the Universal Law of Attraction each of us is constantly drawing to us the conditions that fit our thoughts. Whether we are conscious of it or not, this law is always operating.

That is why it is so important to keep our minds on what we want and not on what we don't want. Whatever our conscious 'gardener' sows into our subconscious 'garden' will be reaped later. Remember, your dominant thoughts become your reality. Always be aware, therefore, of that which you affirm to yourself because, through constant repetition, whatever that is will become the truth of what you believe and live by. When we internalize something by constant affirmation and repetition – for example, 'I am very creative' – our subconscious mind causes us to act accordingly.

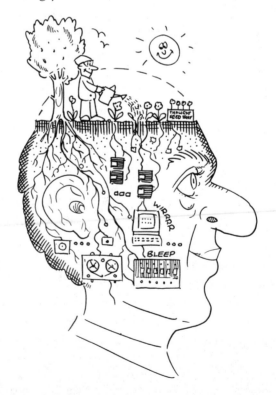

Through the operation of our thought forces we have the creative power to manifest in our external world what we think about in our internal world. If the majority of our thoughts are thinking about what we should or should not have done or be doing, or could or could not have done or be doing, then we manifest a reality of anxiety and guilt. And in this reality we never seem to get clear enough of the mire even to take a breather.

Yet to behave in this way is the simpler course of action. It is difficult but essential to let go of thoughts which have any negative connotation. Otherwise, keeping them alive causes them to send out stronger vibrations which in turn attract the corresponding physical manifestation. In letting them go you gain power over them, you see them for what they are and can concentrate on listening to your inner guidance, your intuition.

Intuition

Intuition is the spiritual conduit for your inspirations and is absolutely unerring in its guidance. There is no lock, or even door, to this conduit. The only requirement is to be receptive to its flow. You have to expect to receive this flow, however, and the degree of how clearly and plainly you receive this flow is in proportion to how true you are to yourself.

When we are being somebody for everybody we cannot trust ourselves and consequently are unable to trust what our interior guide says. Intellectual pride, prejudices, preconceived opinions and beliefs build a barrier of opinionated dialogue that stands in the way of true wisdom.

Inspirations and creative thoughts are lost amid the internal dialogue of our other selves.

Although intuition is rapidly becoming a key element in business thinking, it is still regarded with much scepticism, particularly by strategists, analysts and planners. After all, it is not easy to admit that a major strategy decision was developed from a few lines scribbled at five o'clock one morning before going back to sleep.

In an ambitious survey of 1,300 senior managers in nine countries set up by the International Institute for Management Development in Lausanne, over 60 per cent admitted that they now used intuition more than logic and reasoning. However the word is defined, intuition remains intensely personal to each individual, although it is recognized as a universal ability. Whatever options you choose to access your intuition, it is important to remain open minded to what you receive. Men particularly must remain open to the intuitive side of their nature.

Women generally have a more developed sense of intuition than men. At one time in his life Henry Ford the second was said to have discussed all major decisions with his widowed mother, whose experience of business was strictly limited. Perhaps men should consult their partners when they get home and ask what decision they would take? In the days of the two-career family, the chances are that couples have less time for each other's work problems, although certainly more understanding of them.

Insight

Insight is by far the most valuable stage of our creative think-ing process. After we have gathered information together and thought about it a great deal we may suddenly receive a flash of illumination – we see the light, the answer we were looking for is created. 'Eureka!' we exclaim when the answer comes after we have struggled with a particular problem. In that moment we suddenly connect two things that were previously unrelated. The punch line at the end of a joke, for example, takes the listener into an area which was previously unrelated until the storyteller makes a relationship. This relationship is completely accepted and totally apparent after it has been made. It is the unusual connection, however, that makes a successful joke.

The story of the great mathematician Archimedes is the classic example of an insight flash. He was an advisor to the tyrant of Syracuse, King Hiero, who was suspicious that a gold crown he had commissioned was not made entirely of gold and silver but also contained lead and base metal. Archimedes knew the specific weight of gold and silver but required the volume of the crown as well as the weight in order to solve the problem. While taking a bath he noticed how the water level rose when he got into it. He suddenly realized that he could measure the crown's volume by immersing it in water and measuring the displacement. He ran through the streets of Syracuse shouting 'Eureka!' Archimedes put his solution down to an intuitive or super-conscious solution.

Velcro, penicillin, X-rays, Teflon, dynamite, the Dead Sea scrolls, iodine, smallpox vaccination and quinine all owe their discovery to intuitive inspiration. The world has progressed because of these inspirations, because of individuals who have taken the time to listen to their inner selves, who have taken the time to consciously sit and mull over ideas as opposed to

hustling and bustling and dealing with life by trying to find external ways to sort things out.

Two major stumbling blocks to your creativity are comparison and competition. Your uniqueness sets you apart from all others. There has never been another person like you, and never will be, so what is there to compare or compete with? The majority of people measure their success by comparing themselves with others. But genuine success is what you do with your own potential. It is not to be compared with what other people have already done with theirs. All comparison can do is break down the limitations in our own minds. It shows that if something is achievable by one person it is achievable by another.

Once one person had broken the four-minute-mile barrier, formerly believed impossible, literally hundreds soon followed. We are now even approaching the three-minute mile. When individuals show what can be done they are like all true leaders of the world who have shown what is possible when you are yourself and able to become a channel for an Infinite Source. Gandhi claimed to be no more than an average man with less than average ability. He said: 'I have not the shadow of a doubt than any man or woman can achieve what I have, if he or she would make the same effort to cultivate the same hope and faith.'

Comparison makes you feel either superior or inferior – both are expressions of your ego, your limited thinking.

If you need to compare to make yourself feel a little better, then you are saying someone else is not good enough. If you put others down, you may think you raise yourself up. But what you are really doing is putting yourself in a position to be criticized by others. We all do this on some level and it is good when we are able to transcend it. Becoming enlightened is to go within and shine a light on yourself so that you can resolve whatever darkness is there.

Everything changes and what was once perfect may not be any more. In order for you to keep changing and growing, you must keep going within and listening to that which is right for you in the here and now – the present moment.

SEVENTH: A Sense of ...

LEADERSHIP

Imagine a glass full of water. Now pour the water into a vase, then pour the water from the vase into a cup and then into a jar. The water has found itself in a glass, a vase, a cup and a jar, all of different sizes and shapes. Yet, regardless of what it was in, the water retained its original nature – the container had no effect on it whatsoever. So it is with you.

Realize your true and original nature and you will always be in command of yourself. The true nature always knows whether counsel from others is true or false, sensible or nonsensical, which is why your main task is reunion with your original self. It is a paradox that the best leaders are the best followers, and when you follow your own inner guidance you become your own leader.

Communication

The development of leadership attributes is interrelated with the development of what you are and what you can do. Leadership is about what a person is (character) and what a person can do (competence). And to the degree that you channel these factors in a mission, and live by it, you communicate to others who choose to follow you. Leadership is about communication. Leaders are not self-appointed and leadership cannot be enforced. Only authority is enforceable, and even then, not for long. Leadership is a transaction entered into and maintained voluntarily and is based on mutual trust, respect and communication.

When living by the example of developing character and competence, everyone can develop leadership attributes. It follows therefore that everyone has the innate ability to be identified as a leader in his or her particular field or circumstance. The mindset, however, in the Western world does not see it this way. The Eastern mindset holds that true leaders do not intervene unnecessarily, but their presence is felt. Their role is to facilitate, not control, others' progress, enabling them to say at the end, 'we did it ourselves'. In the West our experience and beliefs in our search for evidence of leadership has misled us to see only leaders. Our paradigm of a leader is one who is highly visible, a special and rare individual that we can put on a pedestal and knock off again later when our expectations change or we see things differently. An authentic leader, however, does not always grab the centre spotlight but stays more in the background.

**Leadership is a commonplace activity
that can be developed in ourselves.**

In looking for that which we expect to see we do not always realize this. Leadership is not based on theory or technique but operates under simple principles. You will only attain true leadership when your people say you are their leader, and to become a leader you have to develop essential characteristics.

Adhering to the underlying theme of this book – development from the inside out – you cannot expect to lead and direct others before you can lead and direct yourself. In order to do this you must see if you can be a follower, for the quality of a

leader is in direct proportion to the subordination of the ego. A moderate ego demonstrates character and wisdom. Egocentric leaders can get carried away with themselves and, as they become superstars, the teacher outshines the teaching. Individuals who are able to follow as well as lead allow others to have the floor. They do not seek to take all the credit for what happens and have no need for fame.

Yet by 'letting go' they inspire even more loyalty from others. This is the paradox of 'doing less means being more', or 'you let go in order to achieve'. Individuals who seek credit and use others in order to make themselves look good do not endear themselves to others and resentments begin to grow. You become impressive when not trying to impress. And you teach others more effectively and develop loyalty through the quality of your silence rather than the chatting and boasting of those who seek or need to impress.

The wise leader is like the water in the analogy at the

beginning of the chapter. He or she always responds in the same way, regardless of circumstance, and without complaint. Water is fluid and responsive. It never fights but flows around the obstacles it meets. The authentic leader is yielding, like water; there is no need to push and those following cannot resent or resist.

Leadership Paradigms

Where leadership seeks to release the potential of others and provide guidance, the common paradigm is that a leader, in the form of a manager, needs to exert control and direct. I believe that this paradigm has misled us for you cannot manage and control people without constructing an impediment to their growth. You manage things, but you lead people. Yet people are treated as things, and things to be made more efficient at that.

People prefer to be led than to be managed. Management is for administration whereas leadership provides inspiration. Successful leadership means communicating a mission so that it makes sense to others. Its inspiring yet meaningful message should create that flash of illumination when everyone says 'Of course, now I see it'. In this way it becomes the way forward developed by others. Otherwise any vision remains a dream without the involvement of others, and a leader without followers is not a leader at all.

Leadership can empower a group of people to successfully follow a common purpose. The only effective way to do this is to develop the full potential of others. Effective leaders exude energy because energy comes easily when you love your cause. The same things that get you or me excited and cause us to do outstanding work will cause others to do the same. This is the important thing for leaders to remember, that the people who are part of their team are in fact very much like them.

The enormous changes currently being experienced throughout the globe demand a style of leadership so completely revolutionary that it challenges all our existing paradigms. Obsolete management paradigms need to be superseded with a principle-based, high-quality effective leadership paradigm, a model for thinking and acting. A paradigm for 21st-century leadership is rooted in seven key factors without which it cannot be successful.

1 Alignment to universal principles

2 Shared values

3 Inspiring vision and mission

4 Empowerment

5 Planning

6 Team building

7 Continuous study for character and competence development

Alignment of universal principles, shared values and inspired vision and mission are linked by integrity, the supreme quality for a leader. Regardless of the organization or situation, no real success is possible without unquestionable integrity. Being true to yourself comes naturally if you live by your mission. To have followers and gain their confidence, effective leaders must not only believe in their mission, they must be seen to believe it – to literally 'walk their talk'. Anything less instils cynicism and disillusionment and a 'them and us' attitude.

Uncompromising integrity and ethics – a commitment to do things right – make up the steel reinforced concrete foundation on which other leadership qualities build. If you don't have integrity and are building on sand, followers will become bogged down in the mud-slinging that inevitably ensues and renewed control will be necessary. The only way that people can believe in a business is if it is an honest place to work. Equally important, the only way people can believe in a management is if their leaders display impeccable integrity and tell the truth. As we understand and take action based upon the greater good, we become more respectful and tolerant of one another.

Our values are our teachers for the future. As business moves into an era characterized by less direction from authoritative figures and fewer procedures, more than ever we need to rely on the guidance that shared values provide. Both mission and values stir us at the deep emotional and spiritual level. They should be the underpinning for every decision and activity in any organization. Through effective communication release and guidance, individuals become their own leaders following their own judgement.

Each individual can make a difference and play the leadership role when empowered to do so. Empowering leadership means bringing out the energy and strengths people have and getting them to work together in a way they would not do otherwise. Empowerment starts in the heart by genuinely knowing and caring about people. The essence of real empowerment is respecting that each individual is important and can effectively contribute valuable input if believed in.

Instilling a sense of power in others is a delicate balance between distributing leadership responsibility and helping build self-esteem, knowledge and mastery. This starts with trusting people's competence and judgement. So the primary task is to bring out the very best in people by educating and mentoring them. Empowerment is about sharing ownership and allowing people to make mistakes and to learn from them. For this environment to flourish it needs to be within the framework of an effectively communicated mission.

Effective leadership will mobilize people around a mission that urges them to do their best. In understanding a common purpose, they then have a clearer idea of what they can contribute. The mission allows people to produce in concert as they exercise their own judgement and realize their full potential. Only when understood by your company will a mission ignite dedication, high performance and commitment to excellence.

Only those individuals who literally 'walk their talk' will provide this understanding through their effective communication as leaders.

Successful leaders are the catalyst for galvanizing everyone towards a common purpose. This is achieved by developing leadership in individuals.

We must invest wisely in leadership for both current and future generations in order that rewards expand beyond business into our families, communities and society at large. We must act as role models, influencing by example and inspiring our teams to tap into their enormous potential, challenge conventional ideas, take risks in pursuit of dreams, create enthusiasm for accidents and focus on missions.

Our society is in many ways at a cross-roads – tremendous crises need to be faced but at the same time there are windows of opportunity for enormous breakthroughs in traditional thinking. These will occur only to the degree that more and more of us from every segment of society live by principle, see ourselves as leaders, stretch beyond our current paradigms and comfort zones and commit ourselves to making a greater contribution.

Rename or Reframe?

Perhaps the most effective way of commencing to develop a leadership paradigm in individuals is to break with tradition and change the name 'manager'. What's in a name you might ask? Plenty. Names can have a dramatic influence on our perceptions, and consequently on our attitude and behaviour. A name can literally spawn a paradigm. The name De St John-Stevens conjures up different perceptions than the name Bloggs, regardless of the background, occupation and particular character of the two individuals.

If you are a manager do you remember what it was like when you first became a manager? You started to see everything differently didn't you? The same problems you complained about before, you saw differently as you assumed the responsibility to resolve. Having a new name and position is the fastest way to shift someone's paradigm. With a new paradigm your behaviour and attitude change dramatically.

Think of other paradigm shifts in your life. What happened to your paradigm of life when you moved from being single to being married, or from being married to being divorced or separated? Do you remember how you perceived things differently with a new map? Do you remember viewing your responsibilities differently after each promotion in your life? What happened when you became an aunt or an uncle, grandparent, mother or father? Did you recall the new name, perceive a new role and experience a fundamental change? A new paradigm is a revolutionary change. Titles have their own paradigms – a producer creates, a manager controls and a leader guides.

The old name of 'supervisor' has been superseded by 'front-line leader', Boss has been superseded by Managing Director, Chairman or Chief Executive. 'Manager' or 'controller' has stayed and 'leader' is now only used for a head of state. It is almost as if we have an aversion to being referred to as a leader – and, perhaps, to the responsibilities that go with this. More importantly, perhaps, is it because a leader cannot be named but has to be chosen?

Do you prefer, or like, to be managed? Do you enjoy managing others? Or do you prefer to be led, to follow a leader? And wouldn't you rather lead than manage? Management, as opposed to leadership, more often than not creates a delusion of control. It often seeks to make the future as predictable as the past, to restrict change and to maintain the status quo.

The term 'supervisor' as a description of what the job entails is today obsolete. So is the word 'manager'. 'Leadership' is better than 'management' and is much more satisfying to both leaders and followers. But even if the name is not changed its connotations can be reframed to create a new paradigm. If we focus our attention on techniques, on specific 'to do' lists, on current pressures, we will make only minor gains. But to make quantum leaps in our effectiveness we need to shift our paradigms by reframing our title in our own minds. In this way we will see the situation that we are involved with in totally new ways which perhaps we had not previously considered.

People do not want to be just managed, they want to feel that they are contributing to worthwhile goals. They want to be part of something, with a mission that transcends their daily tasks. No one wants to do work that has little meaning throughout a whole working life. We, as striving organisms, want purposes and principles that lift and ennoble us, inspire and empower us and lead and encourage us to be the best we can possibly be.

The Principle-Based Paradigm

The current human resource paradigm transcends previous forms of human relations and authoritarian paradigms of the past. But it is now time for even this model of thinking to be transcended. The human resource paradigm sees people as the main resource of an organization – not capital assets, not physical properties, but people with hearts and minds that can be developed to make efficient use of their creativity, strengths and ingenuity. This is excellent, but a principle-based paradigm works in a more holistic way. As well as seeing people as resources and assets, it also sees them as spiritual beings. Individuals want meaning and a sense of doing something that matters.

Using this paradigm we can lead people by a set of guiding principles – the natural laws and governing social values – that have characterized every great society and every responsible civilization throughout humanity. Leaders who manage by principles see that people have greater creative energy and initiative than their positions presently allow.

To release creative energy you need to treat the employee behind the desk in the same way as the customer in front of the desk.

This attitude brings out voluntary commitment from another, the kind of voluntary commitment that is impossible to purchase. This type of thinking leads not only to the increased efficiency continually sought but, more importantly, to enormous steps forward in personal and business effectiveness. You will have more of the bottom line when you care for the top line, your people. They are your customers and they in turn will treat the external customers – the ones who provide the bottom-line figures – in the same way as you treat them.

The Management Paradigm

I am not suggesting that we have no more managers, as confusion and chaos would result without systems and procedures. It is the thinking which needs to be reframed. There are three essential roles in every organization – Producer, Manager, Leader – and each one is vital to the success of the whole. But in many organizations the thinking processes are biased by the management paradigm. Management deals with establishing structure and systems, and focuses on speed to market, efficiency, cost benefit analysis, filling the gaps of weaknesses. But it does not deal with direction or keeping a mission in sight. So how effective are efficient systems if you are heading in the wrong direction?

The point I am making is that regardless of managers' efficiency, expertise and skills, if they do not embrace voluntarily the full impact of why they are doing what they are doing, how effective are they? Managers who cannot communicate by their example why they want others to do the same, will need to exact more control over teams to ensure that systems are followed. Anything that cannot be communicated effectively cannot be understood as intended and consequently will not be bought into.

The degree to which a manager leads by example is in direct proportion to the effectiveness and increased efficiency of the team. To the degree that a manager operates under a leadership paradigm, people operate from the paradigm of making a valued contribution and not from a 'it's just a job' or, worse, 'I only work here' paradigm. New thinking and reframing often need outside stimulus. It is important to walk in other people's worlds from time to time.

Catalysts for Change

Continuous education and study act as stimulus, but too many read only the trade and professional journals and papers relevant to their own business. If you surround yourself with what you do, how will you receive outside stimulus? Remember, ideas which cause monumental change and progress come from outsiders on the periphery with nothing to lose. Take time to read works of wisdom, study other cultures, and enjoy art and travel. These activities need to be cultivated by business, not frowned upon as indulgences. Often they can trigger off ideas and act as catalysts for growth.

Ideas come from various sources, and to think in terms of leadership it must become part of a company's responsibility to push people into these other worlds. Otherwise there is a danger that the company will start to suffer from the syndrome of restricted and fixed ideas that is regularly associated with group in-house thinking.

In addition to reframing certain individuals who have a more fixed way of seeing things, some may need mentoring to guide the release of their hidden strengths and thus their effectiveness. Leadership thinking follows the principles of patience in developing others.

Principle-centred leaders understand that regardless of how

individuals, team members or family members construe their world, they all have – and want to offer – an effective contribution.

Seeing three 'f's can be reframed to seeing six 'f's and light-bulb energy can be focused and directed to laser-strength energy. Major organizations must extend leadership thinking to embrace the cathedral philosophy. If the craftsmen who created those buildings had been impatient to receive a result during their lifetime, what would those structures look like today – if they were still standing, that is?

**Leading for the sake of power and
building for the sake of ego cannot sustain
the trust of those it touches.**

Leaders must shape and share a vision which gives meaning to those who follow. Trust in others is repaid by trust in them as the mission becomes their mission and their own ideas are taken into consideration. A cathedral is a shining example of something created by generations of individuals who shared a common purpose.

Total Quality

There were once two Arab boys, Yazid and Haroun, who became close friends as they shared boyhood adventures in the village and desert. The passing years separated them, with fortune making Haroun a great sheik while Yazid became a poor rope maker.

One day while selling his ropes in a street in Baghdad, Yazid came face to face with Haroun. The delighted sheik offered his boyhood friend a position in his court as the royal date merchant, which Yazid accepted. Only the very best dates in the land were good enough for the sheik's kitchen so Yazid's task was to find and buy only superior dates.

A week later Yazid returned on his camel with a load of dates which he believed were of fine quality. After sampling the fruit and finding it inferior, the sheik's advisors wanted to discharge Yazid. But when hearing this, Haroun gently shook his head. 'You do not understand Yazid,' Haroun told his advisors. 'He has lived in poverty all his life, consequently he has no way of distinguishing good dates from bad ones. He truly believes he has a load of excellent fruit, but that is only because he does not understand what he is about. We must be patient with Yazid.'

Sheik Haroun then instructed his advisors, 'Each day I want you to give Yazid a few dates for dinner. Start with a low quality and gradually give him better dates. His own taste will show him the difference. Then I guarantee you Yazid will bring us only the very best fruit.'

The sheik was right. Because Yazid truly wanted more knowledge, he was soon able to raise his standards and serve both the royal court and himself only the finest of dates.

This story illustrates how a leader can act effectively when he holds more of an appreciation and an understanding of how an individual construes the world. Because someone does not see something straight away, the six 'f's for example, does that make him or her wrong or a fool? Haroun's thinking was focused on developing and educating an individual's potential, whereas his advisors (managers) were only concerned that their criteria had not been met. The story also illustrates how subjective quality can be.

So, what exactly is total quality? Is it not like beauty, only held in the eye of the beholder? The greater the development of character, belief, love and genuine pride in the production of something, the greater the quality derived.

But developing individual character will only build greater subjective quality. Developing competence, attention and meaningful contributions within the framework of a mission will bring about the necessary objective quality, for it is not until we can see what we are capable of that we can improve quality. Leaders draw attention to available qualities and do not misjudge initial inability for long-term ineffectiveness.

Leadership attributes guide us to release our potential to learn, discern and earn effectively. If we raise the expectations of others through our expectations of them, we raise their excellence. So many people suffer from low self-esteem that this has got to be one of the greatest wastes of natural resources. It is interesting that whenever you ask immigrants to this country why their children do well they answer 'because of hard work'. In contrast, British parents credit their children's success to talent or luck. When children believe they have the ability to fulfil expectations, they will live up to similar expectations throughout their adult life. To be a real leader with your children, regardless of their ages, teach them that achieving is the result of effort, much more than ability. How do you do this? By encouragement, assistance, coaching and example.

The Natural Way

The most natural way to influence is by example. The order of development in nature is production in spring, growth in summer, harvest in autumn and storage in winter. Managing leaders must also follow this development pattern – producing, growing, harvesting, and storing or consolidating – for to oppose it brings inevitable decline.

  The way of nature as detailed in Eastern philosophy is the overall guideline for human leaders.

You become a leader through natural development, not through learning techniques.

Those who are able to nurture what nature has produced in a way that will inspire others are indeed true leaders. When grass is choked it rots, when trees are choked they are eaten by worms, when people are choked they become ill, and when an organization is choked a hundred problems arise at once and danger and chaos cannot be stopped.

  When an organization is choked it means that the favours of the leadership do not extend to the employees and the wishes of the employees do not come to the attention of the leadership.

- The authentic leader has the diligence to be leader, but not the desire to be leader, thus allowing everyone to fulfil his or her wishes.

- The authentic leader has the position of leadership but not the ambition of leadership, thus allowing an atmosphere without tension.

- The authentic leader does not lead for the sake of money or praise, yet nevertheless receives both in abundance.

- The authentic leader does not pretend to be special as he or she knows that no one person is better than the rest of humanity.

- The authentic leader is principle-centred and not self-centred and uses the minimum of force to act effectively.

- The authentic leader avoids egocentricity and emphasizes being rather than doing.

- The authentic leader has a light touch, is not heavy handed, will neither attack nor defend, and will know to look at both sides of any situation (you cannot see clearly through a window that has only been cleaned on one side).

- The authentic leader pays equal attention to all disputes and is aware of prejudices in judgement.

- The authentic leader looks to what is happening rather than what might be happening and isn't. By being more aware of what is actually happening this leader can do less yet achieve more.

- The authentic leader does not indulge in pretending or faking knowledge but says 'I don't know'.

- The authentic leader knows that the reward for doing the work rises naturally out of the work.

Ten Vital Ingredients

The major ingredients in the recipe for developing leadership are:

1 *Integrity and ethics*: derived from alignment to principles, clarification of values, and continual personal and professional development.

2 *Purpose and goals*: derived from establishing a personal mission statement for your life, aligning it with what you do and setting goals within the framework of that mission.

3 *Energy and enthusiasm*: derived from doing what you love and believe in.

4 *Courage and level-headedness*: derived from the understanding that progress means making mistakes.

5 *High effort and sense of priority*: derived from knowing that you don't die from hard work at a job you love, only from hard work at a job you hate. When number one priority is finished, do not go on to number two. Go instead to a new number one. Why? It is human nature that if you work on number two as if it is number two, and number three as if it is number three, there is a large drop-off in quality as the day progresses.

6 *Non-conformism and self-reliance*: derived from knowing yourself, understanding yourself, trusting yourself and being true to yourself. When you begin to have confidence in your own feelings and act on them you become self-reliant. When you are self-reliant and enjoy this self-trust you no longer worry what others say about you because you are your own person.

7 *Perception and patience*: derived from knowing that what is perceived by you may not be perceived by others and that

only through patience, mutual awareness and understanding can this happen.

8 *Appreciation and empathy*: derived from knowing that the 'I' can only be truly developed through others. Appreciating others' views and empathizing with them is the substance and depth of long-term relationships.

9 *Conviction and commitment*: derived from knowing that conviction is a more powerful ingredient than any other method, and that commitment is the measure of your involvement in what you believe in. Your actions should match the strengths of your beliefs.

10 *Love and attention*: derived from knowing that love for others and attention to their needs is the most potent energy in existence. The only things we never lose are the things we give away.

Ambition

The only way to keep the goodwill and high esteem of the people you work with is to deserve it. Each of us eventually is recognized for what we are – not what we try to be.

No one can create a feeling of mutual trust overnight. It takes time and effort. And sincerity cannot be turned on and off like a tap. People immediately get suspicious of a leader's motives when he or she suddenly makes a big effort to be nice to them.

The right motives are more important than the right moves. Leaders who are sincere do not have to advertise the fact – it is plain to see in all that they undertake and soon becomes common knowledge. Most people want the same thing from their leaders – we all want someone who is honest, truthful and straightforward; someone who really has our interests at heart, someone we can trust.

**In the long run, no techniques, no matter
how clever, can conceal the motives
a person has in his or her heart.**

We must be ambitious to survive, but the human desire to succeed is one thing, preoccupation with personal ambition that keeps us constantly wound up, frustrated, and fretting about our future prospects is another.

Being ambitious for the company or group is by far the best way for leaders to show their talents. If greater rewards and advancement are possible, this is the way to get them – not by resorting to personal ambition with all its side effects of envy, office politics and internal feuding.

Loyalty

The greatest pleasure and greatest pain within leadership is that of loyalty or disloyalty respectively. The deepest cut to Caesar must have been from seeing rather than feeling Brutus's action. The key to loyalty is deserving it – and showing that you do. Individuals who receive loyalty are those who give loyalty and who appreciate colleagues' and friends' viewpoints, problems, hopes and ambitions.

They are individuals who give and share credit liberally and shoulder the blame responsibly. They are sincerely and genuinely interested in the welfare of those who follow them, and deal with them openly, honestly and fairly. These leaders constantly develop their people.

It takes all this and more to earn loyalty. Most of all, what you do must be done unconditionally.

**Whenever you do something for another
on a conditional basis, do not expect
loyalty as a reward.**

You will be disappointed as loyalty does not work like this, and that is probably why many complain about a lack of loyalty rather than striving to deserve it. Loyalty can be had but has to be earned – you have to decide whether you consider it worth the price.

Practise What You Preach

Some people feel that when they have attained a position of leadership at executive level, they are no longer subject to the same standards they expect of others. They think it is their job to tell people what to do, regardless of whether or not they do it themselves. In preaching one thing and practising another you are influencing in an adverse way. Leadership, remember, is communication – it cannot not influence.

Strengths and weaknesses of a company, family or group reflect the strengths or weaknesses of the man or woman who runs it. Walk into a business and within five seconds you know the energy level of the organization. People – customers and clients – can tell within seconds how much your team members enjoy working with you or how much you enjoy working with your team.

When you have difficulty getting people that you work with to measure up to the standards you insist on, take a second look at yourself – are you applying these standards whole-heartedly in your own work, or just preaching for the benefit of others? If you are usually late yourself, how can you expect others to be on time? What is good for the goose is good for the gander, and effective leadership means understanding that that is the way people are. Others will only buy into something if they can clearly see that you have already bought into it.

The way to master principles of leadership and make them part of you is to keep them constantly in mind and live by them until they become second nature. The more you live by and the more you apply the principles of good leadership, the more effectively you can lead others. People have minds of their own and it is their perceptions of the world that make them decide to move or not to move, to be motivated or not motivated by what we do to influence them. The more sensitive we can be to others, the more we can know how they see themselves, and how they see us and the things we say to them or offer them.

When people are led, linked by a common purpose that is important and meaningful to them, they become more confident in who they are and what they can do. When people believe that their contribution is valued they begin to develop courage to act as themselves. In this way they naturally evolve to act-ually become their true selves and in this medium are able to channel effectively their previously submerged nature – a nature which is infinitely more powerful than the false illusions they hide behind. People become their own leaders when they are in command of themselves. You become your own leader when you become true to yourself.

EPILOGUE: A sense of ...

BEING

On a prominent hill near the ancient city of Troy there stood the statue of an archer. The archer held a bow and arrow in his hands, as if ready to shoot. Legend says that the arrow pointed in the direction of a buried chest which contained great knowledge. The chest supposedly contained scrolls and letters that revealed the answer to man's life upon earth.

Over the years many men tried to follow the course indicated by the pointing arrow, but failed to find the treasure of wisdom. But one year a man with a daring mind came to study the situation. The first thing he realized quite clearly was that all the old methods for solving the mystery were quite useless. He therefore determined to think about the problem in a new way.

Many volunteered that it was pointless to seek further as everyone had already tried. Unconsciously they fought to persuade this individual to be more like them and simply enjoy the story of the legend. Some even resented the fact that he seemed in command of his own thoughts and actions. Some questioned why he should feel different to the way they thought. Most were amused because they had seen and heard it all before. However, all of them had a sense that this person was being himself, regardless of whatever any of them thought. They were also aware of having a grudging feeling of respect for this.

In his fresh and individual state of mind, the man patiently sat and watched the statue. He sat with his eyes and mind open and looked for something either obvious or unusual or different. Each afternoon at three o'clock he noticed that the shadow of the arrow pointed between two distant mountain peaks. At the base of those peaks he found the treasure of knowledge he wanted so zealously. From that day on, all who made an earnest attempt to think in a new way towards a problem found the wisdom they wanted. The individual was always remembered by the townspeople with a sense of admiration for having been his own man.

To the degree that we are in command of ourselves we become our own creator. Ideas in the form of insights and inspirations flow to us in direct proportion to how much we become our own person. This we can achieve if we continuously work at being conscious of why we think and act in the way we currently do. The only way to change what you see in life is to change the person doing the seeing; you are what you see. Command of yourself and your life means one thing and one thing only – oneness with yourself and your life – and the sure way to do something about your future is to do something about your present.

Only when you have made sense of yourself can you make sense of the surrounding world. Character development naturally develops your conscience and this provides guidance in harmony with Universal Principles. Let your conscience tell you if you are following a principle or not by taking the time to think why you are doing something whenever you feel uncomfortable about it. Be aware of the stressful signs which indicate that you may have a principle working against you instead of for you. Practise living by principles with no concern for results, for a planted seed is quite capable of developing in the dark.

Encapsulate everything that is important to you in your personal mission statement and promise yourself to adjust and review it as you grow into your own true being.

Everyone experiences flashes of insight, inspiration and

brilliance. Lack of confidence prevents us from believing or acting on them. On the rare occasions that we do we are surprised. Why? And why should they be rare? Because we only occasionally allow ourselves to relax enough to be ourselves. Dawning realizations of what to do become more frequent as we grow more in tune with our true self.

Skills become second nature when practised, but our natural strengths are part of our first and true nature. All of us have a very powerful creative ability within us. It is there to provide us with the inspiration to develop fully what each of us has to contribute to fulfil our potential. It is as important to develop what is part of our first nature as it is to develop a skill which becomes second nature – if not more so.

The wisest and most valuable advisor stays with you throughout your life – you. Even though we often choose not to listen to this advisor it never leaves us and it takes every opportunity to give to us whenever we are just being ourselves. It cannot be clearly heard when we are trying to be someone else. Perhaps when we relax in a bath, at one with our own thoughts, we present our advisor with the ideal opportunity to guide us. So you know what to do. Take time to bathe in your thoughts. Take a bath. Perhaps that is what is meant by 'cleanliness is next to godliness'. Of course, that's it – Eureka !

Bibliography

Adair, John, *Effective Leadership*, Gower, 1983

Barker, Joel A, *Discovering the Future: The Business of the Future*, Charterhouse, 1989

Baron, Robert, *Psychology: The Essential Science*, Allyn and Bacon, 1989

Brown, Mark, *The Dinosaur Strain*, Innovation Centre Europe Ltd, 1993

Burke MD, Richard M, *Cosmic Consciousness*, Citadel Press, 1993

Clarke, J J, *Jung and Eastern Thought: A dialogue with the Orient*, Routledge, 1994

Clason, George, *The Richest Man in Babylon*, Penguin, 1988

Cleary, Thomas (trans) *The Book of Leadership and Strategy*, Shambala, 1992

Cleary, Thomas (trans) *Instant Zen: Waking up in the Present*, North Atlantic Books, 1994

Cleary, Thomas (trans) *Thunder In The Sky*, Shambala, 1993

Cleary, Thomas (trans) *The Essential Koran*, Harper Collins, 1993

Clifton, Donald and Paula Nelson, *Play to your Strengths*, Piatkus, 1993

Covey, Stephen, *The Seven Habits Of Highly Effective People*, Simon and Schuster, 1993

Covey, Stephen and Roger Merrill, *First Things First*, Simon and Schuster, 1994

Dalai Lama, *Freedom in Exile*, Cardinal, 1990

Drury, Nevill, *The Elements of Human Potential*, Element, 1989

Easwaran, Eknath, *Gandhi The Man*, Nilgiri Press, 1978

Easwaran, Eknath (trans) *The Dhammapada*, Arkana, 1987

Emerson RW (edited by Carl Bode)*The Portable Emerson*, Penguin, 1981

Fisher, Mark, *The Instant Millionaire*, New World Library, 1990

Foster, Timothy R V, *101 Great Mission Statements*, Kogan Page, 1993

Goldratt, Eliyahu M, with Jeff Cox, *The Goal*, Gower, 1993

Gracian, Baltasar, *The Art of Worldly Wisdom* (translated by Christopher Maurer), Mandarin, 1993

Gross, Richard, *Psychology: The Science of Mind and Behaviour*, Hodder and Stoughton, 1987

Hammer, Michael and James Champy, *Reengineering The Corporation*, Nicholas Brealey, 1993

Handy, Charles, *The Age of Unreason*, Arrow, 1990

Heider, John, *The Tao of Leadership*, Gower, 1986

Hughes, Vernon, *Esoteric Mind Power*, DeVorss and Co, 1980

Jung, Carl C, *Psychology and the East*, Ark, 1986

Jung, Carl C, *Synchronicity: An Acausal Connecting Principle*, Ark, 1985

Keyes, Ken, *Handbook to Higher Consciousness*, Love Line Books, 1990

Kuhn, Thomas S, *The Structure of Scientific Revolutions*, Chicago Press, 1970

Kwok, Man-Ho (trans), *The Illustrated Tao Te Ching*, Element, 1993

Lancaster, Brian, *Mind, Brain and Human Potential*, Element, 1991

Lyttleton, Edith, *Our Superconscious Mind*, Philip Allen, 1931

Mascaro, Juan (trans), *The Upanishads*, Penguin, 1965

Mascaro, Juan (trans), *The Bhagavad Gita*, Penguin, 1962

Naisbitt, John, *Global Paradox*, Nicholas Brealey, 1994

Ouspensky, Peter, *The Fourth Way*, Arkana, 1986

Ouspensky, Peter, *Tertium Organum: The Third Canon of Thought*, Arkana, 1990

Ouspensky, Peter, *Conscience: The Search For Truth*, Arkana, 1990

Palmer, Martin, *Taoism*, Element, 1991

Peck, M Scott, *The Road Less Traveled*, Arrow, 1990

Price, Frank, *Right Every Time*, Gower, 1990

Rawlinson, J Geoffrey, *Creative Thinking and Brainstorming*, Gower, 1981

Scovel-Shin, Florence, *The Game of Life and How to Play it*, Fowler, 1984

Shoemaker, Sydney, *Self Knowledge and Self Identity*, Cornell University Press, 1963
Waitley, Denis, *The New Dynamics of Winning*, Nicholas Brealey, 1993
Watts, Alan with Al Chung-Lianng Huang, *Tao – The Watercourse Way*, Arkana, 1993
Wilde, Stuart, *Whispering Winds of Change*, White Dove International, 1993
Wu, John C H (trans), *Lao Tzu's Tao Teh Ching*, St Johns University Press, 1961

Further Reference:

The Syntopican of The Great Books, edited by University of Chicago, Britannica Inc, 1986:

Vols 1 and 2: *The Great Ideas*	Vol 16: *Copernicus*
Vol 6: *Herodotus and Thucydides*	Vol 28: *Galileo*
Vol 7: *Plato*	Vol 35: *Hume*
Vols 8 and 9: *Aristotle*	Vol 42: *Kant*
Vol 12: *Marcus Aurelius*	Vol 53: *William James*

Index

About the Author

Bestselling author, Colin Turner is an internationally acknowledged leader in the field of human potential. Combining Eastern philosophy and contemporary Western experience into a practical format for daily use, his thought-provoking books and lectures blend Universal Principles and Spiritual Growth with the commercial realities of life. His programmes, and books which include *Born To Succeed*, *Financial Freedom*, and *Made For Life*, have inspired people worldwide and his principled approach to business has been embraced by leading organisations.

For details of other inspirational works by
Colin Turner
please write or call:
The Catalyst Group
1 Berghem Mews, Blythe Road, London W14 0HN
Tel 0171 603 7779 Fax 0171 603 2220